Harry and Magda

The Story of Our Family

by
Wesley G. Pippert
(with lots of help)

Hog Press

Hog Press
an imprint of Culicidae Press®
PO Box 5069
Madison, WI 53705-5069
USA
culicidaepress.com
editor@culicidaepress.com

HOG PRESS

HARRY AND MAGDA: THE STORY OF OUR FAMILY
Copyright © 2024 by Wesley G. Pippert

No part of this book may be reproduced in any form by any electronic or mechanized means (including photocopying, recording, or information storage and retrieval) without written permission, except in the case of brief quotations embodied in critical articles and reviews. For more information, please visit culicidaepress.com

ISBN: 978-1-941892-88-6

Library of Congress Control Number: 2024945575

Our books may be purchased in bulk for promotional, educational or business use. Please contact your local bookseller or the Culicidae Press Sales Department at +1-515-462-0278 or by email at sales@culicidaepress.com

x.com/culicidaepress — facebook.com/culicidaepress
threads.net/culicidaepress — instagram.com/culicidaepress

Designed by polytekton ©2024

The Pippert Family

To Harriet
whose fulfillment is yet to come

Table of Contents

Introduction — 8

Chapter 1 Portland — 11
  The Families — 12
  Progressive Club and Charivaris — 17
  The Country Schools — 18
  Nora Springs — 19
  Mason City — 20

Chapter 2 The Alliance Gospel Tabernacle — 26
  The Preachers — 29
  The Families — 32
  Medicine Lake and Weddings — 35
  What was the Influence? — 36

Chapter 3 The Pipperts — 38
  The Great-Grandfolks — 44
  The Pelzers — 45
  Grandpa and Grandma — 46
  The Uncles and Aunt Ruth — 51
  The Other Pipperts — 55

Chapter 4 The Halsors — 57

Chapter 5 The Folks — 73
  Mother — 73
  Growing Up — 74
  As Mother — 77
  Daddy — 86
  Growing Up — 87
  Mother and Daddy — 96
  The Golden Years — 98

Chapter 6 The Older Three	**103**
Lois, Chuck, and Pauly	103
Lois	106
Chuck	110
Paul	117
The Next Generation	123
Lois	123
Chuck	124
Paul	125
P.S.	125
Chapter 7 We Younger Four	**126**
Marie	127
Wesley	135
Harriet	143
Harold	147
Epilogue	151
Marie	151
Wesley	152
Harold	152
Chapter 8 Life Together	**154**
California	154
Back to Iowa	155
The Ladwig Place	155
The Home Place	157
Appendix	**168**
Chronology	168
Daddy's Letter to His Family	175

Introduction

I wrote this book for my children Elizabeth and David and all their cousins. This is what I want them to know and remember about our family. I also wrote it for my brothers and sisters — and me. I have been told that it is too idealized; this may be true. I tried to include the warts — or at least to allude to them — but not to dwell on them for our true story is one of triumph.

Gordon Sabine, former director of the School of Journalism at the University of Iowa and my professional mentor, was the impetus for this book. He said it needed to be done. The project took exactly a year. Initially, I relied on my recollection. Then I fleshed it out with details from my diaries and scrapbooks, and finally, I dug out my letters (I've never thrown any away) and reread Mother's and Daddy's letters to me from the 1950s while I was at the University of Iowa and on my first jobs. Paul, Marie, and Harold offered lots of details and corrections that I had missed. Several of the grandchildren offered their recollections, too, and I have included them as written. But the overall perspective is mine.

I am reminded of what I heard the late Abe Fortas testify at the 1981 hearings into the roundup of Japanese after Pearl Harbor during the dark days of World War II. During the ceremonial opening day of the hearings, the few surviving federal officials from that period testified, and Fortas was among them because he was an assistant secretary of the interior at the time. "I have no idea why I have been called to testify," Fortas said, "because I always left an office with the only thing I brought to it — my hat," a reference to the officials who leave a post and take with them truckloads of all their files. "Furthermore," he said, "like my law partner told me the other day, I'm at an age where the things I remember best — probably never happened!"

My reward came from my nephews and nieces and their own recollections. Paulette wrote, "Doing this brought a few tears, some laughs and memories of a very happy childhood. It also gives me an opportunity to say how important my family is to me." Gary wrote, "It is a powerful, moving account. You had me grimacing, reading sections out loud to Karen, and introspecting about my own past on Grandma and Grandpa's farm. You've told our story for us, and I'm grateful for all your work on it. Its value will outlast your life and mine."

Wesley
Washington, 1990

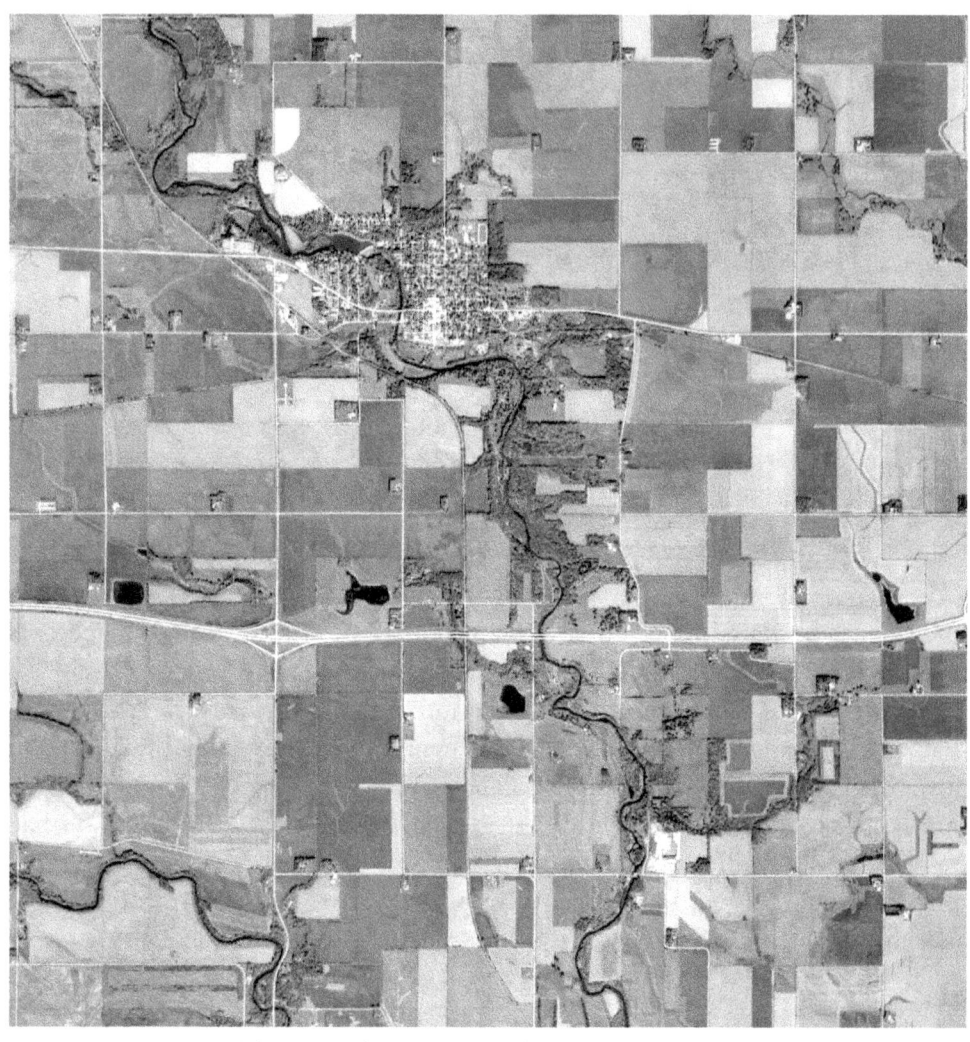

The Winnebago River and Mason City, Iowa

Chapter 1

PORTLAND

> Yes, we'll gather at the river,
> The beautiful, the beautiful river,
> Gather with the saints at the river,
> That flows by the throne of God.

The Winnebago River flows southeasterly through Mason City and beyond. At an outcropping of limestone beyond the Taylor Bridge four miles east of US 65 and one mile south of old US 18 lies Portland. It is fitting that Portland, Iowa, the smallest of the nation's plethora of Portlands, is midway between Portland, OR., and Portland, ME.

It is not much of a village now. The Portland elevator's two huge silos fill the skyline. That's about all.

It wasn't always like that. The Portland of the early 20th century was a bustling place. A young teacher from Mason City, Magda Halsor, commuted to and from the depot. Mrs. Sweet, the station agent, would stand next to the tracks and wave a flag, one color for the train to pass on through, another color for it to stop. Now the depot is gone. The mill, along the Winnebago where Miss Halsor used to take her pupils on picnics, is gone. So is Portland No. 6, one of the schools where Miss Halsor taught, and where her three eldest children, Lois, Chuck and Pauly, attended later. The Portland elevator has merged with the Plymouth elevator.

Old Mr. Hubbard used to ring up sales of pennies, nickels and dimes back at the Portland store in the '20s and '30s. Mrs. Davidson really modernized it by eliminating the old gas lights in favor of a single bulb drop light, unshaded and hanging from the center of the high ceiling. That done, she sat in a chair chatting with customers. The store is gone, and, of course, so are Mr. Hubbard and Mrs.

Davidson. The Portland Hall — "the Hall," actually owned by the Woodman's lodge — where the Portland church and Portland school plays were held and other social gatherings met, has been torn down. All of the missing landmarks were post-World War II casualties. Portland is a shadow of its former self. John Emmert recently put up signs just on the edge of town saying, 'PORTLAND: Next two exits.'

In the Portland community, the two axes are US 18, running east and west, and the Portland-Plymouth road, north and south. US 18 during those early days was known as 'The Pike;' the Mason City-Nora Springs road was one of the first stretches of paving in the state. The Plymouth-Portland road was gravel for years; now it is blacktop.

THE FAMILIES

Of course, it was the people who really made up Portland — the Emmerts, the Bauers, the Krauses, the Ladwigs the Pippers. They threshed oats and filled silo together, went to revival meetings, and married each other. It's impossible to keep the relationships straight. Tragically, much of the rich lore as far as our family is concerned went to the grave with Mother, Daddy and Lois.

Way, way back, more than a hundred years ago George Emmert married Jane Bauer. They had two sons: Ben (3/29/1887-7/13/65), who raised purebred Poland China hogs and had a fancy hog house with a furnace in it, and Frank (3/23/1889-5/14/65), a saintly man who was a dairy farmer. They lived on a fine farm one mile west of our place on what became new U.S. 18. It had a big white barn, that hog house, and a big square stucco house and the small, frame original house. I don't know of a man whom Daddy respected more than Frank. Frank was recognized· as a spiritual giant in the Alliance Gospel Tabernacle although he slept through every sermon. Mother carefully explained that Frank worked very hard. Frank occasionally preached at the church when the minister was absent. Both Frank and Ben married women named Maude. Frank didn't marry until he was 56, when he took Maud Robinson as his bride. Mrs. Ben Emmert, nee Maude Currier, had taught Daddy. Ben's son John stayed on the home place; son George, Paul's good friend, made his career at the cement plant.

The Bauers lived on old U.S. 18, less than a mile from us. Art and his wife, Gertrude McLeod (1879-1970), a stately, gentle woman who was one of a few college graduates in the neighborhood, had four children, Lynn (2/12/05-5/?/65), Kenneth, Wilma, and one daughter, Dorothy, who married Wilbur Kellogg. The Bauers also adopted two grandsons, Robert and Russell, who were children of their late daughter, Wilma Brown. In her early years, Art Bauer's wife, Gertrude, taught Daddy in school at Portland No. 3 on old U.S.18, the site of the KSMN tower where Paul was a member of the maiden staff in 1947. The big white Bauer barn was the last of the big dairy barns built in the immediate neighborhood, probably in the 1940s, although the barn on Harold's farm south of Portland was built in 1958. Wilbur Kellogg, Art Bauer's son-in-law, operated one of Mason City's several dairies in the original barn. One evening Doc Bascom of Nora Springs, who was nearly blind, was speeding along old U.S. 18 and struck a John Deere tractor operated by the Tevis' hired man, Henry Beard. The impact was so severe that the rear wheel was knocked off the tractor and rolled down the pavement into the Bauer yard and landed up against the barn where Sam Clifford was milking cows. It killed Beard, one of a large number of traffic fatalities in the Portland community over the years.

During the late 1940s and early 1950s, Gertrude Bauer's grandsons, Robert and Russell, tried to run the small Bauer farm themselves. One spring, actually in June and almost summer, the Bauer boys still had a field of corn stalks along the road from the previous year that hadn't even been plowed. So Robert would plow about twenty feet of ground, disk it, drag it, and plant it, or, he might just plow it and plant it skip the disking. Then he would do another twenty feet. To everyone's astonishment, he got the field done. Russ, through Paul's influence, went into radio. But everyone wondered about Robert Price and Esther Tevis (Esther 1893-1966 was a sister of Art Bauer) who lived across from the Bauers and the KSMN tower site. They had three boys — Evan and Ellsworth, better known as Jake and Skunky, and Marlin. Jake and Skunky, and Bob Lindsey, who lived a mile straight east of us, were classmates of Marie in the class of 1947 at Nora Springs High School. Price (1891-1974) also farmed 80 acres between our place and Portland 2. Frequently during harvest time, Price, hauling corn wagons behind his John Deere, would stop and give me and Harriet and Harold a ride down to our road.

Frank Krause (1863-1955) farmed along the Milwaukee Road tracks. Daddy used to say that when a storm was brewing, he'd keep an eye on old Frank in a nearby field — when Frank quit and headed for the yard, the storm was soon to strike. Frank Krause was a big operator — and he ran his John Deere until he was 85 years old. Frank's only son-Elmer (1893-1958) became Cerro County

Triple-A chairman after World War II. Elmer had three sons known far and wide for their laugh and delight. But as adults, their mirth turned to bitterness. Billy (1928-60) died at 31 and Jack and Bob never speak nowadays, even though their farms adjoin.

Elmer's sister Jesse (1904-?) married Hugh Hughes (1897-1974). Jesse had been a student of Mother; Hugh was perhaps the only farmer in the neighborhood at that time with a degree from Iowa State. They were our next-door neighbors on the west for nearly 20 years and surely rank as our favorite neighbors over the years. Their son Frank became a veterinarian and Joan became a nurse on the West Coast. But Helen Hughes (1928-53), a dietitian, died at 25 of diabetes, and I was one of her pallbearers.

We were related to the Krauses in the way that folk around Portland are related. Frank Krause's wife Elizabeth (1867-1947) was a Freese, and her brother Will (1872-1954) was married to Ella Pippert ·(1878-1965), a sister of Grandpa Charles Pippert. Will was a mean sort, and he later was committed to the county home to live out his days. The Freeses had two children. Audrey (1910-58) was killed when her car plunged into the Winnebago near Taylor Bridge, and Johnny (1917-) stayed on the home place. He opened the grave for Daddy in 1976, appropriate since they were cousins.

There were others. The McEacherns were reputedly the richest family in the Portland community; sand and gravel pits were found on their farm that were mined profitably and they went on to own a big hunk of downtown Mason City; Miss Halsor once dated Glen, as she had once dated Elmer Krause. McEachran place actually looked pretty typical and even a bit run-down; the only clue to the wealth was the big, new machinery in the yards. Glen McEachran (1893-1987) was the oldest remaining farmer from his generation in the Portland area when he died.

C.W. Files was a one-time state legislator who lived just south of McEacherns, and as a widower, he married a widow, Mrs. Wilhite. Later, Uncle Calvin bought the Wilhite place, which was torn down to become the campus of North Iowa Area Community College (NIACC) in 1969. Harold bought the old Files place from the Huffs. And there were the Ladwigs, the source of the richest family lore, so rich that they will be treated later on.

Another source of lore were our next-door neighbors to the east — old Pete Steil (1863-1949), his bachelor son Clarence (1895-1974), his widowed daughter Alma Thogerson (1893-1974), their cleaning woman, Mrs. Steeve, and her son, Richard. (Three others of our closest neighbors also died in 1974 — including Price Tevis and Hugh Hughes, as well as Aunt Esther and Aunt Phyllis.) Alma

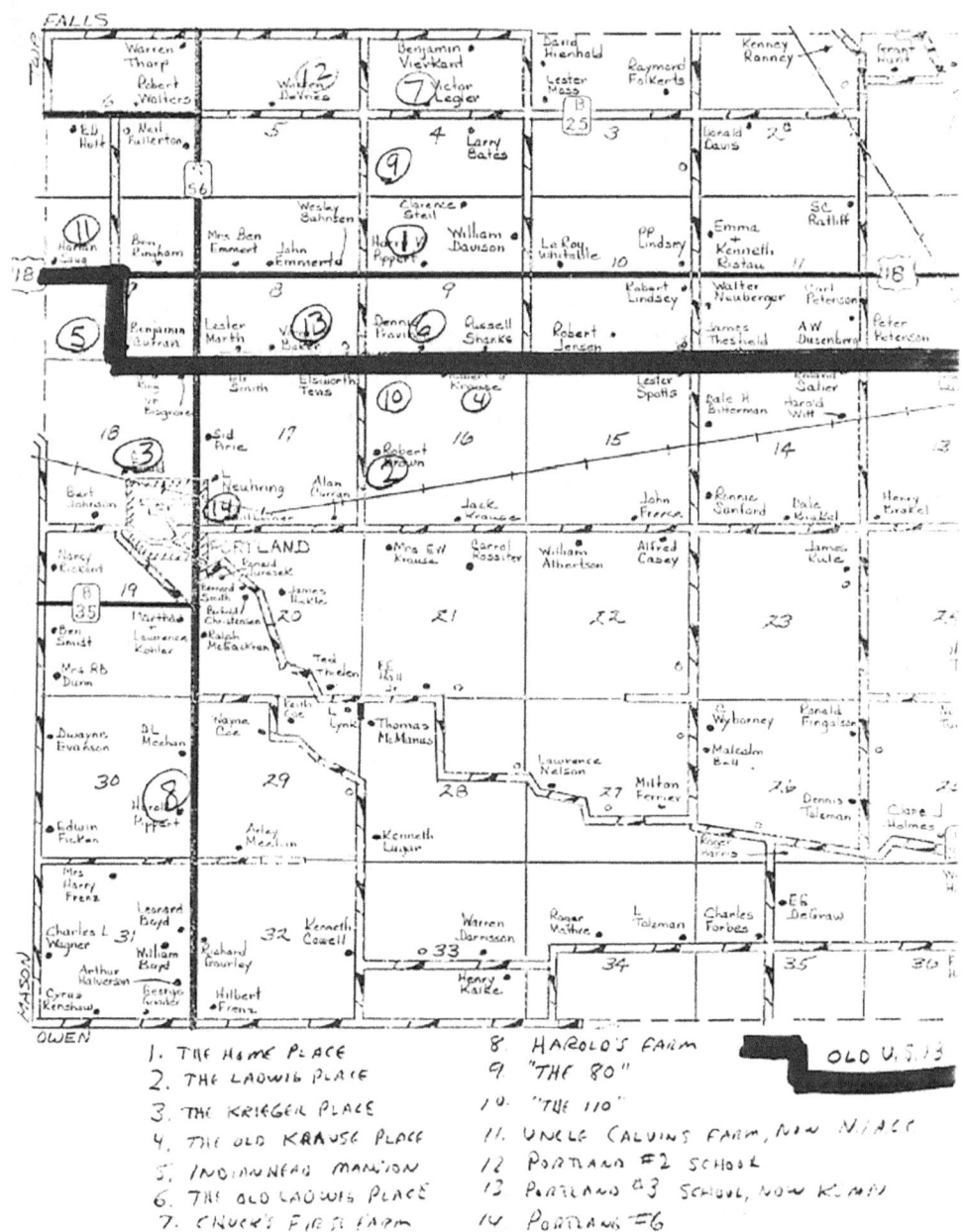

1. THE HOME PLACE
2. THE LADWIG PLACE
3. THE KRIEGER PLACE
4. THE OLD KRAUSE PLACE
5. INDIANHEAD MANSION
6. THE OLD LADWIG PLACE
7. CHUCK'S FIRST FARM
8. HAROLD'S FARM
9. "THE 80"
10. "THE 110"
11. UNCLE CALVIN'S FARM, NOW N/ACE
12. PORTLAND #2 SCHOOL
13. PORTLAND #3 SCHOOL, NOW KLAPP
14. PORTLAND #6

had been married to P.J. Thogerson, a high school classmate of Mother and later one of the top bosses of Jacob E. Decker & Sons packing plant in Mason City. Steils' place, up in the field, was ram-shackle, and Paul more than once refused to eat the noon dinner there while threshing or filling silo.

The Steils had a reputation for being notorious fabricators of the truth. They had an aging row of box elders on both sides of the road, which while adding a sylvan touch to our road, also provided us with electricity outages every storm when a big branch would fall off and onto the power lines. They also plowed against the line fence that ran north and south between our two farms, so that, as the years went on, the level of their ground was much higher than the level of ours, making the drainage water gush down on ours and erode it away. When Marie's youngest son, Doug, considered farming after abandoning computers and Dallas, this was the-place he thought about.

They also provided me with a situation over which I feel guilt. Dick Steeve, who was a year or two older than I was, was not liked by the other kids at school. His parentage was uncertain, he got a haircut once a season, he told whopping stories, too. I am certain I behaved toward him just like the others did. He went to Eldora (the state training school) for 10 years at 16 for stealing cars. He was obviously a lonely, lonely boy — and I didn't help.

There were the Grubens — Hank {1906-66), Bud, and Norleda(1909-58), whom Mother always called 'Norletes'. All were big, heavy-set Germans, with an appetite to match — and they died too young. Daddy had the only power-driven, 10-foot binder in the neighborhood and when he went there to cut oats I was delighted. Not only would there be a huge dinner but there'd be meal-sized coffee breaks in mid-morning and mid-afternoon. One night in the 1950s, the rural telephone line (Line 22 — our number was 22F21) rang incessantly, a signal of distress. Bud Gruben's barn was on fire. It burned to the ground.

Norleda married Jim Sandy (1912-), the brother of Mabel, Uncle Calvin's wife. I was fascinated by the interwoven nature of this particular relationship: Mother taught Jim Sandy in school; Jim's wife, Norleda, taught six of Mother's children — Lois, Chuck and Pauly in the Portland school, and Wesley, Harriet and Harold at Portland No. 2. When Harriet was sick with rheumatic fever, Mrs. Sandy tutored Harriet. Mother eventually realized that Norleda was spending most of Harriet's tutoring time sipping coffee and eating Mother's ginger creams.

The Portland elevator was run, among others, by Sime Hill in the 1920s and early 1930s, Chuck Yaggy in the war years, and Dick Talbot, who gave a eulogy at Daddy's funeral in 1976.

Progressive Club and Charivaris

In those days life was much more neighborly and social. One of the main events of the neighborhood was the monthly Progressive Club. The meeting moved from the home of member to member, meaning that each family hosted about once a year. It was great fun. The Krause boys, Chuck and Pauly, George Emmert, Skunky and Jake Tevis, would sit on the staircase of whoever's house and crack jokes and laugh. The meeting time was 8, but the program never began until 9:30, about the time the Krauses were arriving. There was always a roll call, although everyone knew who were present. The roll call was to give an answer to some question, like, "What is your favorite radio (no TV in those days) program?" Pauly answered, "Bob Hope," and I never hear Bob Hope to this day without thinking about that. There would be a program, like a state highway patrolman giving a talk about safety, and the hostess would serve a rich lunch.

And there were the charivaris, the parties thrown to celebrate weddings. During Charley Files and Mrs. Wilhite's charivari at Files' place, one of the boys kept bouncing peanuts off Charley's bald head, which he took in his usual good humor. Another time, during Bob Bauer's charivari, one of the boys — probably Skunky Tevis or one of the Krauses — wandered outside during a melee, reached into the wires on Bauers' tractors, and gave them a yank. Or another typical thing to do was to wait until 10 o'clock or so, when the newlyweds were in bed, and take a board and rub it down the clapboard siding, making as Daddy would put it a "fearful" noise. Or they would take a 12-gauge shotgun and fire it just outside the kitchen door.

There was abundant tragedy around Portland over the years. While he was growing up, Jack Krause got run over by a car and dragged underneath. The axle was much higher in those days; he would not have survived today. Counting Beard, there were fatal traffic accidents one mile west, one mile south, and one mile east of our place. My hunch, those days of gravel roads and little traffic, one simply drove without looking around. To the east of our place, a newcomer to the neighborhood, Mrs. Seiberling, was struck and killed when she pulled onto the road and was hit by a car driven by Junior Matzen, a deaf young man who lived two miles north. In 1948, two weeks after the school year started, Mrs. Sandy was heading north for Portland 2 on the Plymouth Road at the Emmert corner and was involved in an accident in which someone was killed. Two years later, Jeanette Krause was driving down the gravel road toward Portland when Donnie Gruben (1934-50) came cycling out of a field driveway onto the road. She struck and killed him. We have a picture of Mrs. Krause signing the registrar at Marie's wedding a month after that accident. The pain is etched on her face.

I probably got more fun out of the threshing and silo-filling rings than almost anything else as a farm boy. The way it worked was this: a farmer who owned a threshing machine (Pete Steil and Ray Shanks did so; Daddy was in Shanks' threshing ring) or an ensilage cutter would organize a 'ring' of five or six farmers. They all helped each other until everybody was done. Most farmers had a team of horses and a hay wagon, loading them up with bundles of oats or corn, then taking them into the yard to the threshing machine or ensilage cutter. Most farms took a day to complete. It was quite exciting. Most farmers used teams of horses to pull their wagons, but occasionally a farmer would have a tractor on the wagon. When Daddy did that, I often got to go along to operate the tractor. The best part were those incredibly big noon meals — hence the expression, "cooking for threshers" — and mid-morning and mid-afternoon breaks. Before they ate, the farmers, all dirty and sweaty, would line up near the milk house and douse themselves with warmed water, and then wipe some of the water and a lot of the dirt onto a feed sack that served as sort of a rough towel.

Our mail man was Milt Lewis, who arrived every day at 11. We kids would race out to get the mail, and sometimes Marie got there first and in embarrassment I would hide in the ditch in the sweet clover. Milt saw me, of course, and would laugh and make a little joke. One time Milt baled some hay for us, and his two boys, Myron (Lefty) and Darrell (Bill), tied the wires on the baler. They went on to become football and basketball stars at Mason City. Lefty and Duane Jewell, an all-state basketball player, later went on the Mason City police force.

THE COUNTRY SCHOOLS

When I was a boy, Portland Township had ten schools, numbered 1-10, each a typical A-shaped white frame building with a bell tower and two outhouses. Each schoolhouse was heated by a big furnace in the middle of the room.

The biggest, with twenty to thirty pupils, was Portland No. 1 simply, the Portland school. That's where the Older Three went. We Younger Four went to Portland No. 2, about two miles north and a mile east of Portland. Marie was the only one of us seven children who went to both Portland 6 and 2. Portland 2 had a six-stall horse barn out back. Mother's first teaching job was at Portland

2, and for years Daddy was president and Mother was secretary of the Portland 2 school board. Their records are now at the Pioneer Museum at the Mason City Municipal Airport. The folks believed in country schools, and Portland 2 was about the last to close down in Cerro Gordo County, in 1954, but not until Harold had finished. Bart also attended Portland 2 briefly when Lois and Jim were living in Mason City, making three generations of our family to have gone to that school.

Daddy went to Portland 3, where Mother taught later and now the site of station KSMN's tower. His teachers included Maude Emmert, Ben's wife, and Gertie Bauer. In those days some of the boys were in their late teens by the time they finished grade school, taking time out to help their dads farm, and clearly some of those young bucks were disciplinary problems. Daddy once told of such a school that had a new man as teacher. The first day the new teacher took out a big knife. He drew a small circle on the blackboard and then went to the rear of the room and shot the knife straight into the circle. "We'll have no discipline problems here," he announced. And, Daddy said, he didn't.

I don't remember any of those disciplinary problems at Portland 2. I had three teachers — Miss Mullaney through the fourth grade, Miss Quinn through the seventh, and Mrs. Sandy for the eighth grade. We always had about ten pupils. What I do remember is a rather precocious acquaintance with sex. One recess I, then probably 6 or 7, saw Dick Steeve making love to Wanell Dunlap out behind the grove; he was in the second grade, she in the first. And during one neighborhood party at the Klatts, all the adults were downstairs, and the kids were upstairs, and I saw the same two doing the same thing in one of the bedrooms. The Symnes family, who lived on the first farm that Chuck and Billy lived on, had seven children — "and that means my folks have (made love) (not the word he used) seven times," my good friend Melvin Symnes informed me. I didn't get it at the time, but I estimate ninety per cent of what I know today about sex I had learned in country school by the age of 7 or 8.

Nora Springs

In many ways, our community was drawn to Nora Springs, or 'Norie'. That's where J.H. Pippert, my great-grandfather, preached — and his son Charley settled. The story goes that great-grandpa's church was on one side of the street, and another church on the other. One Sunday, one congregation was singing,

"Will There Be Any Stars in My Crown?" and the other was singing simultaneously, "No, Not One; No, Not One." On the Ladwig farm, our mail address was Nora Springs. They banked at First State Bank in Nora Springs. That's where Calvin, Marie, and Harriet went to high school, and where Harold's children attended. That's where Dr. Sowers, our veterinarian, lived. And that's where Doc Henley, who delivered us younger three children, practiced. It's also where the nearly blind Dr. Bascom practiced until 1974 but never filled the void left by Doc Henley.

We loved Doc Henley. He was a slight man with silvery hair who looked like George C. Marshall, and, so gentle, a trait that did not extend to his driving. We used to see him zip by on old US18 heading from Norie for Mercy Hospital in Mason city, obviously his foot to the floorboard. When any of us were sick enough, we would go to Norie, climb the wooden stairway to Henley's office, and sit in his waiting room with the curiously appealing odor of alcohol and medicine. Daddy got the tip of his index finger caught in machinery twice. After seeing Dr. Henley probably a dozen times, Daddy asked for his bill. "Oh, 50 cents," Henley replied.

Even in its busiest days people would park their cars in the middle of the street. Now, Doc Henley and Doc Bascom and the dentist are gone; so is Bright's Corner Drug (Bright drove the school bus all four years Marie went to high school). Volkman's blacksmith shop is closed. So is Tatum's Hardware, and the bakery next door.

East of town lies Park Cemetery where four generations of Pipperts are at rest: Great-grandpa and Great-Grandma Pippert; Grandpa and Grandma Pippert, Mother and Daddy and Uncle Les; and Cousin Marilyn. We boys' and Harriet's plot are there as well.

Mason City

Yet, as the years wore on, Harry and Magda's family seemed more drawn toward Mason City. Mother's family was from Mason City. That's where the Alliance church was, that's where Lois, Chuck, Pauly, Harold and I graduated from high school, where Lois worked at the State Brand creamery and several of us at Jacob E. Decker & Sons packing plant, that's where the folks shopped at Sam Raizes Department Store.

Mason City is the 'River City' of *Music Man,* the musical written by former Mason Citian and shirt-tail relative Meredith Willson. The portrait Willson sketched is quite accurate: the Winnebago and Lime Creek flowed through Mason City; their confluence was in East Park. And Mason city was known for its music.

The main streets were State Street, running east and west, and Federal Avenue, running north and south. Old US 18 followed State; old US 65, Federal. The north-south streets were named after the presidents, in order of service, west of Federal, and after the states, in order of ratifying the Constitution, east of Federal. Thus, a Mason Citian could always remember the presidents' states in order Washington, Adams, Jefferson, Madison, Monroe; or the states, Delaware, Pennsylvania, Georgia.

At the heart of the city was the intersection of State and Federal. On the northeast side was the brick, six-story First National Bank (telephone number '1') where both Uncle Alfred. and Uncle Jess worked. On the southwest side was a building, with low, horizontal lines and an overhanging roof, designed by Frank Lloyd Wright. In the 1950s it housed KSMN, of which Paul was a member of the maiden staff. A block to the north, across the street from Central Park, in the only new office building erected in downtown in recent years, is the Laird Law Firm, headed by Morris E. Laird, the finest lawyer in the area, a friend of Daddy, and the father-figure who handled the family's complicated legal affairs after Daddy's passing. South on Federal a couple of blocks were Sam Raizes Department Store and Myer Wolf's. North of Federal six blocks was — and still is — Birdsall's ice cream, some of the best ice cream I have ever eaten anywhere in the world. To the west is Forest Park, then the fanciest residential neighborhood in the city. Auntie Esther and Uncle Carl lived there. To the north were Mason City's main industries — Decker's, the two cement plants, and the sugar beet plant.

Mason City, I felt, had two things in which there has been tremendous pride. One is the Public Library, beautifully located in a curved building constructed in the early 1940s and equally beautifully located in downtown Mason City in rock gardens along Willow Creek. Nearby, over Willow Creek is a graceful, arched foot bridge — just like in *Music Man*. Actually, the old Carnegie library, located next door to the old high school, is itself a beautiful building.

The other source of pride was Mason City High School, which we always thought was one of the best high schools in Iowa. The Mohawks had fine teams. The 1943 team was undefeated state basketball champion, and the first six players made all-state. But my impression may not have fit reality. When I was at Roosevelt Junior High school between 1947 and 1948, our football team was undefeated and unscored upon, the basketball team was undefeated, and the track team was undefeated with a couple of relay state records. Sounds like it bode well for my high school class? Well, the 1950 Mason City High School football team during my senior year did not even score a point until the third game of the season! Chuck Wolf joshed the quarterback, Chuck Van Ry, about being third team all-conference; of course, only two all-conference teams were chosen.

What was peerless was Mason City's music. To my knowledge the Mason City High School Band has never received anything less than Division I ratings in local, state and national competition. Carleton L. Stewart, a superb cornetist, was the band director most responsible for Mason City's fame. He once turned down the directorship of Indiana University's famed bands. Lois played the violin in his 1937 national contest. Chuck and I played the tuba in his bands. Stewart resigned just before my senior year, 1950-51, to buy Les Reed's music store, and he was succeeded by Paul Behm. Behm had equally good results but with a completely opposite approach. Stewart would select one piece, and we would play that piece and that piece only for a year. It was difficult — Tchaikovsky's "March Slav," Moussorgsky's "Pictures at an Exhibition," etc. By contest time, of course, we had mastered it. Behm was different. We would sight-read two or three pieces during every daily rehearsal, and obviously we learned how to handle a great variety of music. Behm didn't choose the contest piece until two weeks before it was to be held. The results were the same. I played first chair for Behm, and I was in a brass quintet that won first in state.

The first or second week of June was the North Iowa Band Festival. In its heyday, when all the little towns still had high schools, more than 100 bands and queens took part in the all-day extravaganza, with the thousands of musicians playing in a massed concert at Roosevelt Field in the evening. I had never seen a parade anywhere to match it. We boys all marched in it. So did Walter Mondale, he once told me. At one of the festivals in the late '40s or early '50s, Meredith Willson returned as marshal. Now the festival is a shadow of its former self. There are only 25 or 30 bands and queens because of the closing of so many high schools, and the queen is crowned in the afternoon. In 1988, two of our relatives were queens — Harold's daughter Heather was Miss Nora Springs and second-cousin Serena Shields Volstad's daughter was Miss Forest City. One of the most musical families in the community was the Earl Dean family, and to stretch it a bit, we were related: Chuck's brother-in-law (Paul Poppen) and Earl Dean's son Richard married sisters (Amy and Mary Lou Haight).

∽∾

Mason City had a good newspaper, the *Globe-Gazette,* edited by a famous man, W. Earl Hall, and Enoch Norem, and a good radio station, KGLO, a CBS affiliate then and now. The *Globe-Gazette* carried both wire services, and this is how I first became aware of United Press. I used to go to the KGLO newsroom in the Globe-Gazette and read the wires by the hour. I never dreamed I would write as many words for UP as probably any other person.

The *Globe* posted the latest front page outside its old building on East State Street; Daddy would often stop on the way home from church on Sunday night to read it. We listened to KGLO a lot: Keep Time With Damon's, 7:30-8:15 a.m.; Holsum Headlines, 8:15 a.m.; the noon markets; News of the Nation ("The People's Gas and Electric Company, serving North Iowa's city, towns and farms, presents its 3,333rd (or whatever) broadcast of News of the Nation. Now here is KGLO's news editor, Chuck Hilton!"), 6 p.m., and the Evening News Roundup, 10 p.m.

My book, *An Ethics of News,* suggests that the changes in Mason City economically were a microcosm of the revolutionary changes in the nation in the mid-twentieth century.

When we children were growing up, Mason City had jobs. In earlier years, Daddy used to work the season at "the sugar beet," as American Crystal Sugar Co. was known. It was torn down in 1989, including the huge smokestack that loomed over the northern edge of Mason City along U.S. 65.

Lois, Marcella Wang, Lois Gephart, and Francis Emmert from church wrapped butter by hand at the Iowa State Brand Creameries. State Brand was the largest of a half-dozen dairies in Mason City, including George Williams' Sweet Clover Dairy, to which Daddy sold milk, Hartman's Dairy next door to our farm, Wilbur Kellogg's dairy less than a mile away. None of these smaller dairies is now open. In those days every farm had a few milk cows; there are few or none in Cerro Gordo County now. State Brand Creameries is owned by the Associated Milk Producers Inc. (AMPI).

AMPI, of course, was the huge Mexico-to-Minnesota corporation that was created by the various mergers of all these dairies. It grew so powerful that it went to Chuck Colson, White House special counsel during the Nixon administration, to get an increase in the federal price support for raw milk in exchange for a $400,000 donation for Richard Nixon's 1972 campaign.

Decker's, founded in 1899, was a local family-owned firm. Decker Iowana ham was known the country over. Most of us seven children worked at Decker's to help earn money. I did so during three summers, 1952, 1953 and 1954, working first in the by-products department where all the condemned meat, bones, hair and blood — every single part of the animal was used — were crushed, cooked and dried for tankage. The odor was the most foul that I have ever smelled and it simply could not be washed off.

During that summer in by-products, I wore no shirt and a pair of dungarees that were soaking wet with sweat from the 120-degree temperatures. More than one worker pointed out to me that the motors on the big driers faced the open windows, while the tailgates to the driers where we workers pulled out the cooked tankage, were inside of the room. More than one worker pointed out to me the theory for this arrangement: The motors faced out toward the open windows so they could get cooled off, because, they said: "It costs Decker's money to replace a motor that breaks down, but Decker's can always hire somebody else to replace a worker who breaks down."

Decker's was bought out by Armour in 1935, and after World War II by Greyhound buses. The Greyhound headquarters in Phoenix decided the plant was old and decided to close it down. At its peak Decker's had a payroll of 1,300 and a kill of 600. The *Globe-Gazette* carried a story saying the mayor was going to head a delegation to go to Phoenix and persuade Greyhound to keep Decker's open. Good luck, I thought. The predictable result: Decker's was closed in 1975 and is now leveled.

What was Greyhound's obligation to the Mason City community, which had supported and slaved for Decker's for decades? I have no idea how Mason City kids work their way through college now.

Sam Raizes Department Store on South Federal Avenue was central to the existence of our family. Mother and Daddy sold eggs, which were candled by hand (each egg was put part-way into a hole in a box with a bright light inside; this revealed whether the egg was rotten) in JO-dozen crates that helped pay for our groceries and clothes — all at Sam Raizes. All of these items were listed individually by hand in a small account book — for this was before the days supermarket's computerized check-outs. Our bill was generally between $50 and $100.

Sam and his wife had two or three sons who helped in the store — Milton, Leon and Harold. The Raizes were Jewish. Often Mother went to the corner of the store where dry goods were sold and talk with Mrs. Raizes, probably about

God although Mother would be sure to work in Jesus. I am totally unaware of any anti-Semitic feelings in my family and the friendship with the Raizes may have been one of the reasons. Mason City had only two super-markets then — A&P and National Tea. Now it has several shopping malls and numerous super-markets in scattered malls on the edge of town. Downtown seems to me like a weathered, old, abandoned farm building.

As the years wore on, something happened to Mason City. Although the city limits were extended in 1958 east to the Emmert corner, a mile from our home place, the city did not grow, fixed permanently, it seemed at just under 30,000. Worse, there seemed to be little vision, little appreciation of the aesthetic. They tore down the grand old courthouse and moved into the remodeled but hopelessly bland Standard Oil building. They tore down the Music Hall, the first public school building in the nation erected exclusively for music. They turned down several ballots for a downtown auditorium. When they finally approved a shopping mall in the downtown, with a total lack of sense of beauty they built the mall facing north toward the ugly downtown with the parking lot on the south side running along the river, carefully fencing out the weeds on the bank. I had always envisioned a mall that capitalized on the river — River City, remember?

Chapter 2

The Alliance Gospel Tabernacle

As Mother tells it, revival broke out in Portland. It must have been about the time of World War I for Magda Halsor was teaching there at the time. Sinners went to the makeshift altar in the Portland hall, weeping and confessing their sins. Grandpa Pippert was there. So was Frank Krause. Caldwell, who ran the Portland store, got saved and entered the Alliance ministry. And the Emmert brothers, Ben and Frank. Probably Gertie Bauer, later a long-time member of the Alliance. And they were baptized in the Winnebago River near Portland.

Mother said this was the start of the Alliance church in Mason City, although according to the authorized history of the church the congregation was begun while Mother and Daddy were in California in the middle-1920s. But the two accounts do not necessarily conflict.

Actually, there had been an earlier revival in Mason City, probably in the mid-teens. Billy Sunday, the major league ballplayer turned evangelist, held tent meetings and Mother and Grandpa Halsor went nightly. This was when Mother was "saved out of the Lutheran church." At the time she was organist and Sunday School teacher at Trinity Lutheran Church, later one of Mason City's biggest and loveliest churches.

The Alliance Gospel Tabernacle we attended while growing up was anything but lovely. It was a squat, brick building located at 616 N. Delaware in Mason City and looked a little bit like a garage. Grandma Pippert lived her last 20 years just around the corner on 7th Street; we generally stopped over after church on Sunday nights. The most distinctive thing about the tabernacle was the wall-sized oil painting of Jesus and the Lost Sheep that Joe Dahl put on the wall in back of pulpit. It was a major event when florescent lights and a blazing neon sign outside were installed. For years, the preachers lived in a tiny parsonage in the rear of the church until Doc Schweizer's former house on East State Street was purchased in the 1940s as a parsonage.

But the preachers were extraordinary. I remember Lowell Young's announcements even yet — "Sunday School at 9:45, morning worship at 11, young people's at 7, and evening worship at 8. On Wednesday, the young people will gather at 7 to visit the rest homes and then prayer, praise and Bible study at 8." We went to church twice on Sundays unfailingly, generally arriving late for the 9:45 a.m. Sunday School hour. The folks' attendance at prayer meeting on Wednesday night, curiously, seemed to get more regular as the years wore on. In later years, after the children were raised, Mother taught Sunday School and was president of the Ladies Missionary band. Daddy was on the board most of the time, except for the Tieszen era when he was taken off "because he was so busy."

Some scenes remain indelibly etched in my mind. "I have an unspoken request," uttered in solemnity so frequently at prayer meeting. Lowell Young's 'chorus time'. The center-aisle ushering of Marvin Carr and Roland Juhlin, done with as much aplomb as any ushers I have seen anywhere. Every Sunday, about 20 minutes into the service, Ivan J. Wendt (1899-1975) would lead a procession of his family up the right aisle, pause at a front row seat, motion in his wife Bertha, their daughter Glennis, and then son Gene, bringing up the rear, would come, bump his dad in, and take the aisle seat.

At one time or another, Al Uthoff, Tracy Kinsel (both of whom are now dead), Jerome Tieszen, Harriett Hert, were my best friends. My first date, which took place during my senior year in high school, was with Beverly Carr. Unbelievably, she had announced her engagement to Merv Roggow of Spencer at a young people's meeting a few days earlier, and later that evening when we talked about the high school play, she made it clear she'd like to go. So I took her; we stopped at the Soda Grill afterward and then I dropped her decorously at her front door. My friends at the Alliance church were essentially members of the big 1950 Mason City High School class — Julene Adelsman, Mervyl Williams, Daryl Miller, Greta Juhlin, Marcheta Rodberg, and Harriett and Bev. And my own 1951 class — Bonnie Jo Adelsman, I, and Jerome Tieszen. Bill Allos, Ernie Claus, whose brother Carl was the first casualty from the church in the Korean war in 1952. Tracy Kinsel, who went directly to the University of Chicago, graduated two years ahead of me. And later, Wendell Stevens, who won first in the nation in cornet four years running and went to Iowa on a Kinnick athletic-academic scholarship, became chief anesthesiologist at Iowa's University Hospitals.

Harold's friends at the church were: Janet Dahl, Willie Pieterson, Jerome Johnson, the Hert kids, Cathy Gravely, and last but not least, Sandy Ballhagen of Rockwell, a gifted singer, whom he married.

Marie's group included Maybelle Adelsman, Joan Toepher, Bonnie Burnett, Pat Williams, Glennis Wendt.

In Chuck and Paul's group were Wanda McKnight, a cousin of Dorothy Young and later our Aunt Dorothy, Warren Waddell, George Emmert, Roland Juhlin, and Don Williams.

Lois' friends included Dorothy, Lois Gephart, Marcella Wang, Keith and Ralph Williams, Mary Glandon, whom Keith married, Joe Dahl, and Francis Emmert.

Curiously, if my perception of Mason City High School has been one of great music and scholarship, it has been the same for the Alliance church.

The folks at the Alliance made sweet music together. Joe Dahl, who became an Alliance minister, and Dorothy Young, later Aunt Dorothy, sang in a beautiful duet. Joe Dahl and Ralph Williams formed half of the male quartet at St. Paul Bible Institute in the early 1940s. Mervyl Williams was soloist for the St. Paul Choral Club in the 1950s, singing a lusty, throaty "Jesus, Hold My Hand." One rally day — every holiday there was a rally, either in Mason City, Osage or Powersville, a cute little contralto named Lois Krause (?) sang "Precious Lord, Take My Hand," and in doing so, caught Paul's eye. Later, she married Ralph Williams. One Sunday morning, Elaine Adelsman was singing a solo, "Come, Ye Disconsolate," when her voice broke. Right song but wrong moment — her engagement to Bob Peterson had just been broken. A few years later, I took her sister, Bonnie Jo, my classmate and long-time competitor, to the 1952 high school graduation ceremony — one of our only dates, just before the Adelsmans moved to Wheaton and asked her to sing "The Lord's Prayer." And a Sunday or two later, she did. Probably no one sang more often at the Alliance church than Gary Miller did in the 1950s and 1960s. Probably the best singer was, in her day, Ruby Toepfer, whose husband, Don, ran an electrical repair shop on South Delaware. Mrs. Toepfer, an elegant appearing woman, put together a choir in the early 1950s, and the first anthem she chose was her favorite and one of Daddy's 'Ivory Palaces'. The most memorable choirs were those that Lowell Young had on Sunday nights in the late 1940s — all the young people from the 7 o'clock young-people's meeting would parade out of the old parsonage, where they had met, into the chairs on the platform, and he would direct a special number.

I actually learned from Lowell Young how to read music and sing bass. "Just follow the bottom row of notes," he said with profound simplicity. "When the notes go up, sing higher. When they go down, sing lower." I sang in a short-lived quartet with Tracy Kinsel, Harriett Hert, and Mervyl Williams in the summer of 1952. We'd practice — and then go out on a gravel road near the drive-in and neck (it would have been wrong to go to the drive-in theater). Paul also sang in a quartet with Elaine and Maybelle Adelsman and Marvin Carr, and Harold sang in one with Ruth Newton, Willie Pieterson, and Sandy. I have no idea what they did after their rehearsals.

THE PREACHERS

One of the first, in the 1930s, L.A. Perkins, went on to St. Paul Bible Institute to teach homiletics. Then came the first of the two most beloved preachers and their families — Paul Freligh and his wife, Mabel. They had four daughters, Edith, Ruth Marie, Alice Ann, and Carol, roughly parallel in age to Chuck, Paul, me and Harold. I can remember yet the Frelighs driving to the farm, all four doors of the car opening, and the four girls come bursting out. Alice told me years later that whenever she thinks of a farm, she thinks of ours. Chuck and the tall, dark, lovely Edith had their first dates together. One Sunday outside church, someone dared me to kiss Alice Ann. I did. It was my first kiss. We were both 4 (I am happy to report it was not our last).

Daddy used to say that Mabel Freligh was a better preacher than her husband. I never knew growing up that women were second-class citizens in this country. Mrs. Freligh's skill, and Mother's strength, were responsible for my naivete; they were the first feminists I knew and I thought *all* women were like them. The Frelighs had been missionaries in what was then French West Africa and left Mason City in 1939 to return. But World War II intervened and they never made it. They came back — we all had a picnic near Taylor Bridge, while Alice Ann colored in a Greer Garson coloring book and essentially ignored me — and finally settled in the Northwest. Edith became chancellor of a community college in Fresno, Calif., a chain smoker and never married. The girls settled in the San Francisco bay area. Ruth married an Alliance minister. Alice Ann married a surly engineer and became an Episcopalian.

Carol married a LeTourneau heir, Don Peterson, although he once told us: "We don't have any of that money!"

Vernon Gowdy was pastor for two years, and during this period, Chuck joined the Navy. Mother never forgot that, at his farewell party at the farm in October 1942, Chuck took a stand for the Lord, and it was under Rev. Gowdy's ministry. Gowdys had two children — Joan and Kenny. Gowdy was a stern man in some ways, and he told me years later he pushed the piano against the door between the parsonage and the auditorium to keep the likes of old Jay Beck from just walking in unannounced.

The beloved Lowell L. Young, and his wife, Mona, came in 1943 and served seven years. He had been an all-state basketball player at Boone, and he knew Lois and Jim at St. Paul. He was young at heart and a superlative preacher. When his first child, Sharon, was born, he was off playing basketball. Occasionally he got the young people together to play basketball. Daryl Miller fashioned himself as a hard-driving player. Rev. Young would play sort of effortlessly, and then every so often, he would slice through the gang of guys like a streak and score — and then he would just stand back and grin. Mac Dresbach and Daryl were the two rebellious kids in the church at the time, but they loved Lowell Young. He used to drive them to out-of-town games — and feign obliviousness when they stuck their heads out the window in the back seat for a quick smoke. Rev. Young did not have a college degree, so he took classes, and in three years graduated from Mason City Junior College. The first two years JC did not have a basketball team because of the war. His third year, JC did, and he played. In fact, he was one of the high scorers and was captain. One game was played Wednesday night — prayer meeting night — so Rev. Young cut short the service, then dashed to Roosevelt Fieldhouse in time to play the second half. The team went to the state championship finals, and lost, Rev. Young said later, because some of the rest of the team, older, World War II vets, got drunk the night before.

We knew Rev. Young in another way. During Mother's long series of heart attacks in the late 1940s, he spent many a night all night at our house, reciting chapter after chapter of scripture by memory. This was the reason for Mother's full recovery. And years later, when Mother died, it was perfectly clear that Lowell Young would return to preach the funeral sermon, which he did to a full sanctuary with his usual eloquence, tears running down his cheeks. Young actually left Mason City during a crisis. He had dared to oppose the purchase of an organ, and he also had dared to tell one mother that she pushed her daughters too much. Since the people he confronted in these two situations were powers

— the Williams and the Adelsmans — he resigned. During a tearful meeting at our farm, a petition was organized to persuade Young to stay and more than 200 signed it. But he moved anyway. I vowed never to let a day pass without thinking about him.

C.D. Tieszen succeeded Young and he was not anything that Lowell Young was. "Timotee Teet," Paul called him. Tieszen stayed, and stayed, and stayed in Mason City. 17 years, from 1950 to 1967. He was a stern Russian who preached a stern Gospel. He opposed swimming parties at Clear Lake — "mixed bathing," he called them contemptuously. His sermons were biblical, but I never heard one that I thought was interesting or practical. He insisted that divorce was grounds for expelling people from church: his own son later got a divorce.

Marie had begun to pal around with Glennis Wendt, then married to Harold Osborne, a friendly, hapless fellow, not nearly her match in passion. They all went off to the St. Paul Bible Institute at the same time in 1949. The whispers about Glennis always were rampant. When the Rev. Cornelius D. Tieszen first arrived at the Alliance Gospel Tabernacle in 1950, one of his first projects was to investigate the activities of Glennis, and in so doing targeting Marie as a key prosecutorial witness. Tieszen in effect subpoenaed Marie to tell him what she knew about Glennis, which was considerable, and Marie, holding ministers in respect, finally yielded to his demands and told him, whereupon Tieszen made her repeat the charges about Glennis to her face. Marie said that during that summer, the summer of 1950, the same summer she got married, she lost 20 pounds. Glennis, since then, went through two or three husbands; apparently none could satisfy her nymphomania. Her brother Gene, who had been a boy preacher, became a big-time trucking executive in Phoenix.

It seemed that Tieszen gave Harold, particularly, a hard time. Mother used to say how much the other young people cared for Harold, and she believed Tieszen resented it. This was also about the time Uncle Les defeated Tieszen to become C&MA Northwestern district superintendent, which Mother felt only further proved her point. In 1966, during one family problem, into which he intruded himself, I told him that if anything happened to Mother and Daddy because of what he was doing, I would thrash him. It was a rash statement I should never have made — and may have constituted assault.

The next winter, at a time when Daddy was recovering at Mayo Clinic from chemotherapy, Tieszen made an untimely visit to see him. It served only to stir the pot. We refused to let him see Daddy on grounds it would disturb Daddy. A short time later, with us children safely away from Mason City, Tieszen went to the farm to see Daddy. Daddy, ever sensitive, dissolved in tears. Not Mother. She probably talked as straight as anyone had ever talked to Tieszen, and Tieszen had to take it, knowing that he couldn't challenge her spirituality. Mother and Daddy left the church soon thereafter.

They eventually settled in the Hanford Community Church which Harold and Sandy attended. The Hanford church was founded in 1889 and had been remodeled several times, most recently in 1970. It was great for Daddy, for he knew most of its members as neighbors or farmers he had assessed. He was buried there in 1976. Mother never embraced Hanford quite as much, and when she died in 1983, we returned to her beloved Alliance for the final rites.

The list of preachers would not be complete without adding in the evangelists and missionaries. The C&MA emphasized foreign missions, and every year a foreign missionary would come for a convention, climaxed by the taking of pledges. My earliest pledge was for 50 cents. The evangelists came with some regularity. Some, like saxophonist Paul Kenyon and singer C.A. Tindley, were musicians. All had been saved out of a life of sin, and their stories matched. An ex-businessman named W.G. Weston told a story I'll never forget: a Christian woman was married to a man who resisted and resisted her repeated efforts to get him to believe. One day he suffered a stroke, and as he lay dying, the minister rushed to the home and urged him to become a Christian. The man looked up at him, his face blank, and all of a sudden, he started saying "Lost! Lost! Lost!" as his head kept flopping from one side to another. And he died, his head still flopping, still saying "Lost! Lost! Lost!" as his breath ran out. Stories like that, plus singing every verse of "Just As I Am" or "Softly and Tenderly" several times, was enough to get the most hardened of sinners to the altar, weeping uncontrollably.

The Families

The Mason City church went through a series of pastors and slid downhill starting in the late 1960s until it was a shell of its former self. The halcyon days had been during the Freligh and Young pastorates. The Mason City church was supposed, in its day, to have been one of the two best pulpits (along with Wadena, Minnesota) in the C&MA's Northwestern District. It sent 100 young people into "full-time service," that is, as the church defined it, the ministry and missions.

The main families were the Adelsmans, the Williams, the Carrs, the Wendts, the Dahls, the Chester Williams, and the Herts. I never really thought of our family as being one of the main ones, but we were. Uncle Les became Northwestern District superintendent and then Home Secretary in charge of all Alliance churches in the United States. Lois was the first member to become a foreign missionary. Uncle Jess and Chuck were the Nos. 1 and 3 boys to serve in World War II. I was one of the first to go to a secular university. And, of course, Mother had been the first Alliance member in Mason City, joining the 'society', as the denomination was known in those days, long before there was actually an Alliance church in Mason City.

Joe and Olive Adelsman had four daughters — Elaine, Maybelle, Julene, and Bonnie Jo. Joe, a chunky, red-haired man, was a sheet metal draftsman at Pauley's in Mason City and often sang and filled the pulpit. Mother always felt that Mrs. Adelsman pushed and praised her daughters too much, but arguably they were outstanding — good students, musicians, spiritual. "You can't point a finger at them," she would say. Bonnie Jo was in my class, but Elaine was the one I had a decades-long crush on. She became a widow relatively early, and soon after I transferred to Chicago in late 1961, I borrowed Roy and Marie's Edsel one night and took her to a movie. I was so nonplused that I went through a red light in the Loop and almost had a wreck.

Walter Williams, who had a bit of savoir-faire, was the long-time Sunday School superintendent and his wife, Edna, was the long-time pianist. In the church's interim between having only a piano and getting the organ, Mrs. Williams had a solavox — a one-keyboard organ — attached to the piano. Walt delivered bread for Holsum bakery, requiring him to get up at 3 a.m. So he, too, dozed in church. One Sunday, Mac and Daryl were sitting behind him, and as he dozed, each time his head bounced backward Mac and Daryl would instantly cup their hands and raise them as if to catch it. This happened several times, sending Daddy in a nearby pew into near convulsions of laughter.

There were four Williams children — Keith, who married Mary Glandon from the church; Ralph; Don, the rebel; and Mervyl, a fun-loving contralto singer who wanted to be badder than she actually was.

The Carrs were a fine family. Virgil Carr, soft-spoken with an erect bearing, had been an army lieutenant and now was a postman. As Marie pointed out, the Carrs had the same auto license plate as their telephone number — 1610. He and his wife Marge had three children, the prim Marvin, chunky, fun-loving Bill, and Beverly, a splendid girl who I suspected always felt she was in the shadow of the Adelsmans and Mervyl Williams. Later, Virgil Carr, widowed, married Helen Douglas, whose late husband Paul Douglas was the brother of Olive Adelsman and — oh, never mind.

The Herts were a fine family, too. Paul was a mechanic and was one of several brothers who were top Mason City athletes. Ida (1908-1961), his wife, was a Wagner and a sister of Herbert Wagner. Their eldest daughter, Dorothy, was killed by a car as a youngster during the Freligh ministry. Harriett was one of my best friends; after the tumultuous summer of 1952 — when so many of us Alliance young people 'grew up' — she quickly married a church fellow who was her lesser, Martin Moninger. Darrald was lean and winsome and had great potentiality as an athlete — I once saw him throw out a softball runner from centerfield with a straight peg to the plate. Instead, he opted for the ministry. Marjorie, a quiet, spiritual little girl, became a sophisticated big-city young lady. She died in 1990 of alcohol-related problems, spending the last several years with her live-in boyfriend.

There was all kinds of intra-marriage at the Alliance church. Dorothy Young, a lovely, raven-haired singer who sang "Indian Love Call" at many weddings, married Uncle Jess. Dorothy's sister, Irene Young, married Herbert Wagner, who became a minister. Irene's daughter Carolyn Sue and I were junior bride's maid and best man in Dorothy and Jess' wedding. Ida Wagner, Herbert's sister, married Paul Hert. Dorothy and Irene were the daughters of John Young, a kindly, stately man who was chief engineer at Decker's, and his wife Cora. Cora was a sister of Gerald McKnight, another engineer at Decker's and the man for whom I was named. The McKnights had two daughters, Francis and Wanda, something of a femme fatale. And ·Mrs. Waddell and Mrs. McKnight were sisters.

The families at the Alliance church were actually my reference point. I always assumed they were happier than my family, more spiritual than my own, more committed than my own. A few years ago, I happened to see Mervyl Williams, now married to contemporary-evangelical songwriter Otis Skillings. "How's your brother Don?" I asked. "I haven't seen him in 25 years," she replied. Darrald Hert, one of the most promising young men ever to come out of the Alliance church and later president of the senior class at Wheaton and a Presbyterian minister in California, skipped both of his parents' funerals.

Other commitments. I asked his sister Harriett when she had last seen Darrald. "Oh," she said, "I think the last time actually was when you were last here in Miami" — about five or six years earlier. Not see my brother in 25 years? Not go to my parents' funerals? I began to see that my family were more tightly bonded than many of those that I had put on a pedestal.

Medicine Lake and Weddings

Every summer young people went to Medicine Lake, a since demolished campground near the Twin Cities. I had my first crush there (at least the first since Alice Ann), on a milk maid queen from Detroit Lakes named Barbara Jarandson. One summer, Bill Carr and Patsy Williams, who just finished their junior year of high school, went to Medicine Lake. Patsy had been dating Bill's older brother Marvin. Well! Lo and behold, word came back that Patsy had eloped, not with Marvin but with Bill! Mrs. Carr insisted on going through with another ceremony, which Lowell Young agreed to do providing it omitted the vows, which would have been redundancy to the extreme. The newlyweds took a room at the parents Carr. One Sunday a year or two later, at the young people's meeting, Rev. Tieszen was thundering away on the importance of reading your Bible and praying nightly. "What do you do when you go to bed at night?" Tieszen demanded of the nubile young people. At which Pat Carr began giggling uncontrollably.

One time, in the mid-1940s, Paul and Don Williams were at the Medicine Lake camp together, and the week ended — and no Paul. Sunday came and went, and Monday — and Paul still hadn't come home. In my angst, I went to the cob shed and promised God, I would always serve him if Paul came home alive. The phone rang. It was Paul at the bus depot, arrived on the 6:10 bus. Lois and I went uptown to get him. I didn't notice anything, but Big Sister Lois *did* in a flash. Paul's forehead was bandaged, the result of a cut suffered during a car accident in the Twin Cities while with Don.

The Alliance church had its own version of Portland's charivaris. The weddings were held in the tabernacle and the receptions in the YWCA on Adams Street. Frequently, the bride would be kidnapped during the reception and hustled away. After Marie's 1950 wedding, Chuck and Paul had Glenn Hamblen, a city policeman who attended the church, lock her up in the city jail. Meanwhile, Uncle Jess and Daryl and Mac and Beverly Carr's new fiancé, Merv Roggow, kidnapped Roy and drove off in Jess' new pickup. Out in the country west of Mason City near Dresbachs, Jess and Daryl and Mac got out of the pickup, and made Roy take off his trousers and turn them inside out. Roggow, eager to get back to Sunday evening church and Beverly, jumped in the pickup and, taking Roy with him, headed back to town, leaving Jess, Daryl, and Mac stranded — and absolutely furious. I remember yet the three of them irately summoning Virgil Carr out of church. The situation was not helped by Daryl Miller's having a long-standing crush on Beverly (who, I always believed, felt exactly the same way about him).

In the 1940s there were two Sunday School classes that met socially with their families once a month — the Harvesters and the Gleaners. It took me years before I noted the relationship of those names. The Harvesters were made up of Josie and Vernon Dahl and others in that age grouping, that is, married couples in their 20s and 30s at that time. The Gleaners were the middle-aged class at that time, and thus, Mother and Daddy and we children went. Often, we met in the downstairs auditorium of the PG&E (People's Gas and Electric) Building on NW 1st St. for a potluck supper and a program. Chuck was home on leave during the meeting in the dark days of World War II. He had to catch the 10:10 Milwaukee Road train, and so left the meeting early. "Bless Lord, and Make Him a Blessing," the Gleaners sang as Chuck walked bravely out, and Mother cried.

What was the Influence?

It is hard to assess fully the significance of the Alliance church.

I think I actually saw the Alliance church as my primary group. Indeed, from the time I was a junior or senior in high school until after I had been out of college several years and had spent several month-long UPI vacations in Mason City, the Alliance young people were my best friends. While I was in high school, from the time classes let out in May until resuming in September, the only friends I saw were other kids from the Alliance church.

I really do believe that my Christian beliefs were shaped more by Mother than by the Alliance church. There is no doubt that the Alliance church was fundamentalist. We quite knew that dancing, movies, smoking, and drinking were wrong; yet, from Mother we learned that these weren't the real issues in life.

Nor did the Calvinist (once saved, always saved) vs. 'you can backslide' dispute concern us much, for both schools were represented at church. I believe we were of the Armini persuasion, and I remember Mother and Daddy talking about one of Joe Adelsman's sermons in which he said: "You are as much Christian today as you will be when you die."

Just before I left to go to the University of Iowa in 1951, Rev. Tieszen preached a sermon warning what to expect at a godless university. "They'll tell you there are two Isaiahs!" he admonished. I went to Iowa almost defiantly intending 'to stand' for God. I quickly got involved in Inter-Varsity Christian Fellowship, and through IV the skeleton of my belief was fleshed out.

Years later, Lowell Young said something surprising. It was at the time of Mother's funeral in 1983, and he went to see George Miller, Daryl's and Gary's dad, who had not darkened a church door more than once or twice ever. As Lowell Young related it to Becky and me the next morning en route to Minneapolis, his brief talk with George, now advanced in years, turned to faith, and Lowell Young asked him about Jesus. "I have never denied Jesus, I have never denied Lowell Young's Jesus," George Miller said. "I leave it there," he told us. "If he hasn't denied Him he must have accepted Him. I leave it there." That is a remarkable statement for a Fundamentalist minister, but it was typical of Lowell Young. In retrospect, C.D. Tieszen did great harm, to our family and I believe to the church, with his rigid preaching. The history of our family might have been different had Lowell Young pastored in Mason City through the 1950s.

Chapter 3

The Pipperts

The Pipperts are Germans. And proud of it. But maybe the Pipperts are not Germans. A few years ago, a woman wrote me from Tennessee to say that she had seen my by-line, and since her maiden name was Pippert, she wondered whether we might be relatives. I wrote back to tell her of my visits to Germany in search of the family tree, and, indeed, we were from the same area. The woman, Ruth Randol, wrote back, and added that the Pipperts were not actually Germans, but French Huguenots, French Protestants who fled to Germany in the 1700s to escape Catholic persecution. Pippert, after all, does not seem to be a very Germanic name. I frequently find it pronounced "pea-PEHR," very French-like. "The name is French, obviously," Ruth Randol wrote me.

A few days later I was talking by telephone to Paul, and toward the end of the conversation I said to him, "Oh, by the way, we're not Germans after all. We're French." And I told him what the Tennessee woman had said.

"Our father would not have been pleased," Paul shot back with his usual wit.

But the Pipperts surely are German-like. We all have that husky Germanic build. Frequently Daddy and Calvin would talk on the telephone — in German, presumably to assure that we children or rubbernecks on the party line did not understand what they were talking about. The Pipperts went to the Evangelical church in Nora Springs, the denomination that merged with the United Brethren Church in 1946 and then with the United Methodist Church a couple of decades later. But I don't remember eating much of the German menu of sauerbraten, but that may have been because Mother, the cook, was Norwegian. Her ancestry was a source of constant joshing by Daddy of Mother.

❧❧

The first Pipperts we know of were Great-great-great-great grandfather Heinrich Pipert and, apparently, his son, Great-great- great grandfather and Great-great-great grandmother, Otto Pippert, and his wife, Maria Elizabeth Otter, who lived in southern Germany in Niedermöllrich in the late 1700s. According to the baptism book in the Evangelical Reformed church in Niedermöllrich: "In the Parish Niedermöllrich, Felsberg, was born on the 3rd of March 1811, healthy, in the morning at 2 o'clock and was baptized on the 5th of the same month, Karl Pippert, the son of Otto Pippert and his wife Maria Elizabeth nee Otter." The mother's brother, Carl, or Karl, was the godfather.

Karl Pippert, my Great-great grandfather, was the father of J. H. Pippert, my Great-grandfather, whom I saw as an infant in 1934 in Iowa. Several members of that family came to the United States, and Great-great-great grandfather Karl Pippert is buried in a cemetery six or seven miles west of Baldwin, Kansas. This information comes to me via Earl Torneden, a fourth or fifth cousin and son of Lena Pippert Haas, sister of J.H. Pippert.

In 1964, during my trip to the Middle East and Europe, I looked up the Pippert family tree, based on what little detail Daddy and some of his relatives had. The following is the account as I wrote it at the time:

> The state of Hessen lies in central Germany, along the East German border. Its largest city is Kassel, about 200,000 population. The Fulda flows in from the north through its heavily forested hills. What would it compare to in America? Northern Michigan? I don't know for sure, but I was surprised to find it was not more like Iowa. About 20 miles south of Kassel there is a turn off the autobahn to the west. And from the area of this turnoff came the Pipperts.
> I made this turnoff about dusk on Thursday, June 11, and I drove along the winding road to Felsberg, a town along the Eder River, which I recognized from Great-Aunt Ella Freese's yellowed newspaper clippings as the name of the place where Great-Grandfather had gone to trade school. I pulled up, and asked:
> "Kennen sie eine Familie Pippert hier [Do you know of a family Pippert here]?"

No, they didn't know of any Pipperts. Then I mentioned the names of two other towns I had gleaned from Aunt Ella's newspaper obituary of Great-Grandpa, Udenborn and Niedermöllrich. They directed me farther west and I drove four or five kilometers, about three miles, into Niedermöllrich. I stopped at a house where two men were standing outside in the growing darkness. I repeated the question, and one of them pointed to a house just a few doors away. Pipperts lived there! I went over and out came a man, tall, tanned, and medium build, and his son, tall and well-built. Both were farmers — and Pipperts. We didn't accomplish much, although I told them I, too, was a Pippert. I learned little more from them than that they had an uncle, William Pippert, who was a big banker in Chicago about 1920.

An English-speaking young woman with long blonde hair was helpful, and told me about the town I was looking for — Udenborn, Great-Grandpa's birthplace. It lay west. I stopped at a boarding house in Felsberg and started out the next morning.

In Udenborn, a small village with the typical house and barn in the same building and where that morning they were unloading farm machinery into a garret, I met a woman along the street, Mrs. Therese Romer Glitsch. She got in my car and drove along with me, in search of burgomasters and church rectors. Finally, in Kleinenglis, a young minister in a black suit and collar opened the rolls and found the record of Great-Grandpa's birth. I got certificates. Great-Grandpa's mother's maiden name was Romer, and the lady and I looked at each other as if we were long-lost cousins, which we probably were. I took her back to Udenborn and she invited me into her home. She scurried about for some of the best wine she had in the house and made sandwiches and coffee.

Great-Grandpa was born in Udenborn, the hometown of his mother. But he grew up in the town about five miles away where the Pipperts have lived through the years, Niedermöllrich, a little village on the Eder among wheat and sugar beet fields. So, although Great-Grandpa's birth records were in the main church in Udenborn's district, the records for the other Pipperts were in the main church for the Niedermöllrich district. The burgomaster at Niedermöllrich told me the church there did not have a resident pastor, so his son — Günter Itter — directed me. We drove to Lohre, where we met a balding, Yul Brynner-like minister. We made an appointment for the church at 4. Then, we looked at the records — telling of the births and baptisms of the Pipperts for eight generations, back to 1740, when the church records began (or when the Huguenots arrived?), apparently when the church was built.

Günter and I looked at the old gray church — its high-peaked roof and squat steeple — the same place where Great-Grandpa worshipped, and his father, and his father's father. It was simple. Now much of the enclosed church yard was in long grass and weeds. There was the noble record of valor written by the Pipperts of Niedermöllrich. Time and again Pippert men had gone forth to battle, and more than any other family, they had not returned – three in World War I, four in the battles of 1870-71, one in 1814, and two in the last war had not returned. A granite monument in front of the church and scrolls inside the church bore their names. Earlier Günter and I walked through the cemetery, and we saw the names of Pipperts and their marks of distinction. At least one had been a burgomaster, and the burgomaster who preceded Günter's father was Carl Pippert, whom I had met.

Carl and Reinhard Pippert obviously came from another strain of Pippert, going back to 1800. I met Carl's wife, Martha, and Reinhard's wife, Hildegarde, a blonde Angie Dickinson-like woman was one of the most beautiful women I met in all of Europe. Obviously the Pipperts of Germany have good taste in women, too…

One can only speculate on the reasons for Great-Grandpa's leaving Germany and coming to America. Was it frustration at the failure of the 1848 revolutions of liberalism? He was just coming into his teens then, and he left a few years later. Was it the lust for adventure? It's for others to say how strong this trait is among Pippert men. Or did he wish to flee the surroundings of his home life and start afresh elsewhere? One thing I noticed in the Pippert birth records was that so many of the Pippert girls were named Anna Elizabeth. This was the name of Great-Grandpa's mother. It was the name of his father's sister. If I ever have a daughter, I shall name her Anna Elizabeth.

There are several things to consider here: the earliest relative recorded at the church in Niedermöllrich was Heinrich Pipert in about 1740, who spelled his name with only one 'p' in the middle. Was this a mistake in the records, or is this perhaps traceable to the French and their 'Pea-PER'?

According to the official records, Great-grandpa Johann Hermann was born January 24, 1838 (the birthday of my daughter, Elizabeth Marie) and was baptized February 4, 1838. He originally took the name of his mother, Anna Elisabeth Romer, and did not take the Pippert name until his mother married Carl Pippert, then 28, on April 1, 1839. In the record for Johann Hermann Romer, the name Romer is crossed and Pippert is written in, and Carl Pippert signed. So was Carl Pippert the real father or the benefactor of a damsel in distress? Johann Hermann, by the way, was the name of maternal grandfather, Johann Hermann Romer, a farmhand. Elizabeth, said to be beautiful, died at 35. Carl came to America and died in Kansas at his daughter Lena's home at age 87. His granddaughter described him as "very bright, read books." He is buried in the cemetery behind the Evangelical United Brethren Church in Baldwin, Kansas.

What is interesting, almost eerie in some of the relationships, are the frequency of names — Elizabeth, Heinrich, Harry, and Charles. Johann Hermann, or John Henry, or just plain J.H., was the oldest of seven children. Following in order were Johann Conrad, 1840-1922; Magdalene, 1841-2?-1927-8?; Anna Elizabeth, 1845-?; Wilhelm, 1848-?; Heinrich, 1850-?; and George, 1856-?. We know little about the great-great aunts and uncles. It is believed Wilhelm, or William, married a judge's daughter from Denver, and had five children. Heinrich, or Henry, was said to be a sheriff in Topeka and later a harness maker in Alma, Kansas, where he is buried. They had a daughter, Marie. His wife, Carrie Gleich, is buried in Denver. Anna Elizabeth married Fred Schwartz and had five children.

J.H. and Elizabeth Pippert

We know most about the Kansas contingent of the Pipperts, which included Great-great Aunt Lena and Great-great uncle Conrad, J.H.'s sister and brother. Magdalene, or 'Lena', as she was known, settled in Kansas, and married Frederick Haas, a native of Nutenberg, Germany, in 1863. Great-great Aunt Lena died in 1927 at age 86, and her husband, Great-great Uncle Frederick, died in 1925. She had twelve children. Her sixth born, Rosa Elizabeth {1873-?}, who went by 'Rosa', married George Fletcher Simmons and lived in Lawrence, Kansas. They had three daughters, Olga Simmons, a grocer, and Hazel Simmons, a teacher, both of whom lived at 1214 Ottawa, and Iva Palmer, also of Lawrence. Olga Simmons came to hear me when I gave the 1980 commencement address at Ottawa University. She was a committed Christian. She told me years before it became a national scandal that Gary Hart, who was a native of Ottawa, had changed his last name from Hartpence. Great-great Aunt Lena's second eldest, Maria Elizabeth (1866-1943), who went by Elizabeth, married Herman Torneden. The Tornedens'son, Earl Torneden, an undertaker at Pleasanton, Kansas, has been in most frequent contact. In 1950, after Jim and Roy's car wreck en route to Roy and Marie's wedding, Earl Torneden picked them up. Earl and Paul were in frequent touch. Earl made occasional trips to Iowa to keep up with the clan. His son Wayne once came to Washington, and we went to Foundry Methodist Church and our Bible study together. I liked him. We calculated we were seventh cousins.

At least two of Great-great uncle John Conrad Pippert's nine children lived in Kansas. His son, Charles William, had four sons, Elmer, Harry, Frank and Earl. Harry, ?-1975, was married to Dorothy, and Elmer was married to Leona, and both couples lived at 1824 Barker, Lawrence, Kansas, and had an auto parts business.

The Great-Grandfolks

Great-grandpa (J.H. Pippert), who had a goatee, was a circuit rider in the Evangelical Church. He married Elizabeth Brown, a stern-looking woman, who was born in Impchenhum, Ziegenhain, Kurheism, Germany, in 1861. Jacob Albright was one of the leading lights of the Evangelical Church. He was born near Pottstown, Pennsylvania, and Albright College in Reading, Pennsylvania, was named after him. One of the Evangelical churches that Great-grandpa pastored was in Nora Springs, and here his offspring settled and this is why I am writing this chronicle.

J.H. and Elizabeth Pippert lie buried in Park Cemetery in Nora Springs, the first of the four generations of Pippert in that burial ground.

J.H. Pippert had four children: John, Charles W., 1865-1942, Ella, 1878-1965, and Henry. Charles, who was born in Muscatine, Iowa (where I first laid eyes on Becky!) and Ella put down roots in the Nora Springs area. Ella married William Freese, a brother of Mrs. Frank Krause. Bob Krause, my high school classmate, and I used to joke that we were related through his crazy cousin; indeed, Wild Bill Freese did spend the last years of his life in the Cerro Gordo County home west of Mason City. The Freeses had two children — Audrey, who was killed in 1958 in a single-car accident near Taylor Bridge east of Mason City, and Johnny, who did not marry until late in life. When Daddy was buried, it was Johnny who, as an official of Park Cemetery, opened and closed the grave.

Charles W. Pippert, my grandfather, married Emma Catherine Pelzer on June 4, 1896, while J.H. Pippert was pastor of the Noble Evangelical Church in Griswold. She was a member of the Pelzer family there. Years later, whenever Daddy or his brothers would speak of the Pelzers, they would speak of 'Cass County' where they lived in west-central Iowa. 'Cass County' and 'Pelzers' were synonymous.

The Pelzers

The Pelzers were a family of academicians and public officials, probably more eminent overall than the Pipperts. Our grandma, Emma Catherine, 1873-1961, was the third of the eleven children of Henry Acher Pelzer (1841-1/24/1923) and his wife, Sophia Wohlenhaus (1852-1929). Both Great-grandpa and Great-grandma Pelzer were born in or near Hanover, Germany, the daughter of Mr. and Mrs. Dietrich Wohlenhaus. Great-grandpa Pelzer came to America with his parents in 1841 and settled near New York. Great-grandma Pelzer came to America in 1868. Thus, on Daddy's side, at least three of our four great-grandparents came to America from Germany in a 27-year period between 1841 and 1868. So, Henry Pelzer and Sophia Wohlenhaus married in DuPage County, Illinois (Wheaton, perhaps?? It is the county seat…), in 1870 and moved to Cass County the same year. They lived on a farm in section 9 of Noble Township until they moved to Atlantic in 1900. She was a Methodist, although she attended the Peace Evangelical Church.

Their oldest child was William, or 'Will', 1871-1947, of Griswold. Then followed 2. Carlena, or 'Lena', 1872-1949, who was married to a man named Boos, of Cumberland, Iowa; 3. Grandma (Emma Catherine), 4. State Senator Frank Pelzer, 1876-1944, of Marne; 5. Prof. Louis Pelzer, a State University of Iowa historian, 1879-1946, of Iowa City; 6. Cass County Recorder Emil (or as Daddy pronounced, (E-mee-el) Pelzer, 1882-1952; 7. Mary, 10/6/1883-6/1973, who married Fred Schuler of Griswold, and had two sons and two daughters; 8. Annetta, or 'Nettie', 1888-1934, who married Raleigh Saemish, in Milo, Missouri; 9. Ella, 1890-1947, who married Chris Christensen, of Marne; 10. Laura, 1892-1974, who married a man named Holck, of Wapello, Iowa; and 11. Nellie, who married Harry Weyant and later George Burch, of Des Moines. Daddy often spoke of 'Will', or 'Mary Schuler' (in her case, he always tied on her married name), or Emil (E-mee-el). Calvin and especially Earl made a big point of going to Cass County for the annual reunion. Daddy often spoke about it but went perhaps once or twice total. It was Great-uncle Lou we knew the most about. He was the scholar, the professor at the University of Iowa, the secretary of the Western Conference (now the Big Ten) at the time Iowa was suspended for failure to adhere to conference rules, and at the time of his death, the first vice president of the American Association of University Professors. Missing an arm because of a childhood accident, he was married to an artist of note, Mary Weenich, who painted the murals in the old

Hotel Jefferson in downtown Iowa City, where Chuck and Billy once stayed. I used to stop by and see the murals as a student at Iowa.

Much of the following is taken from *Louis Pelzer: Scholar, Teacher, Editor,* reprinted from the *Mississippi Valley Historical Review,* XXXIII, 2, September 1946: His colleagues described him as a "tall Lincolnesque figure" who "stood as a pillar of strength in support of high scholastic standards." His first contribution to the State Historical Society, "The Negro and Society of Iowa," appeared in the *Iowa Journal of History and Politics* (October 1904). Overall he wrote at least three books and many articles. "He lectured more formally than most but in such colorful phrases that America's past became a many-dimensional series of concepts, with shape, sound and even fragrance," said Elmer Ellis of the University of Missouri. "One of the most kindly of teachers, he enjoyed catching a shirker in the act and then, with a straight face below the eyes, loading him down with a laborious extra assignment."

"Pelzer's friendship was not something to be won easily," Ellis said. "But such was the depth of his feeling that once the relationship had been established, it took considerable abuse to destroy it."

All three-and-a-half years I attended the University of Iowa, I did yard work for Prof. George Robeson, who lived only a block from where Uncle Lou lived, and so I saw their home often. Years later, nephew Gary was browsing some old books and found one written by a former student of Uncle Lou's and acknowledged him. It was highly appropriate, because Gary was a faculty member at Iowa State.

Both of Great-uncle Lou's sons were killed in World War II. Parker (1919-43) was lost in a flight from the West Coast and Henry was killed in the Battle of the Bulge. After the second death, Lou died; an autopsy showed his heart was split open. As Mother said: "He literally died of a broken heart." Thirty-eight years after his two-seat Navy dive bomber disappeared with Parker the sole occupant, the wreckage was found in a ravine in the Chatterdown Creek area of Redding, California. His gold watch, a belt buckle, some American Express travelers checks and a tag with the Pelzer name were found.

Grandpa and Grandma

I do not have a clear fix on Grandpa and Grandma. The thing that always jumps into my mind first is, frankly, not a favorable impression — my father, Harry, the eldest of seven, was allowed an eighth-grade education, while two of their youngest, Ruth and Leslie, got college educations. That is far too much differentiation within one family.

Mother used to say that after she and Daddy were first married, they stayed with the grandfolks (why??) and every morning at 7, Grandma would knock on their door and say: "Time to get up."

The grandparents lived on a variety of farms along old US 18 between Nora Springs and Mason City — all within a couple of miles of each other. At the turn of the century they lived on the Old J.H. Pippert Farm, named for Great-Grandpa Pippert and later our home place. Daddy and several if not all of his six brothers and sister were born there. In about 1914 they moved to the Old Krause Place on the south side of old US 18. It once again is a Krause place, for Bob Krause lives there.

According to Daddy's account, Grandpa sold the Old Krause Place in 1919 and rented, then immediately bought the Selle place, which was on a bluff overlooking the Winnebago River and vast expanses of Portland Township to the south. The Selle place became the site of MacNiders' famed Indianhead mansion, still the most beautiful building for miles. Grandpa sold the place in 1927 to General Hanford MacNider, a wealthy landowner (120 Indianhead farms at one time, Daddy said), president of the First National Bank and Northwestern Portland Cement Co., assistant secretary of war and minister to Canada. He was reputed to be the highest-ranking non-career officer in the army. In 1928 the house and barn on the Selle place were moved a half mile east to the Bisgrove place, and MacNider began to build Indianhead. The mansion sat idle after World War II for many years until it was purchased by Gerard school for emotionally disturbed children. Daddy got to see the renovated mansion just before he died; Sandy has taught for many years at the old mansion.

That's the good side of the story. The bad: according to Daddy, when buying the place, MacNider made Grandpa reduce the down payment of $15,000 that Grandpa had put down to $7,000. (I believe this means that Grandpa paid down $15,000 to Selle, but when he quickly sold it to MacNider, the general made a down payment of only $7,000. This meant, apparently, that Grandpa was out $8,000.) "He really clipped poor old Dad, but Dad wouldn't take any of us along, so he took it!" Daddy said. Some of this money Grandpa lent to a real estate agent, Allan F. Beck in Mason City. A few years later, Grandpa wanted to get his money back from Beck. After his parents died, Daddy wrote his brothers and sisters what had happened:

So, I went to Mr. Beck on the matter and the first thing he told me was, 'Harry, the papers are outlawed, and you don't have a thing to stand on.' I admitted it. But I said, 'Father and mother's life savings are all wrapped up here,' and I said, 'Do you think this just right?' Then he said, "If it weren't for you and Magda I wouldn't waste my time. *But if you and I can work this out I'll do something.*' After a lot of lost time from the farm and my work we inherited the properties that you all remember.

Later in the letter Daddy remarked in passing: "We'll say here after I got all those properties in Dad's name from Mr. Beck: our old Dad gave me $5."

Picking up Grandpa and Grandma Pippert's various moves, they moved back to the Old Krause Place, then to what became the Gruben farm on the crest of the hill just east of Portland. In about 1933 or 1934, they moved to the Old Ladwig Place on the north side of old US 18, which is where Loyd Bartlett and his family of three girls lived while we were growing up, later purchased by Mason City attorney George Marty. Here Aunt Ruth married Uncle Arthur in May 1934, a few days after I was born. While Grandpa and Grandma were living on the Old Ladwig Place, Mother and Daddy lived on the 'new' Ladwig place less than a mile to the south.

In about 1937, Grandpa and Grandma retired. They moved to the Millington place, a lovely acreage on US 18 just east of the Taylor Bridge. The Millington place had one of my favorite houses of all my life. It had running water, the first bathroom toilet I ever flushed, and the first bathtub I filled (Grandma told me to keep it to an inch or two of water, and to this day when I bathe, I don't fill it much higher than that); a fire place; a pantry. We used to stop by on Sunday nights on the way home from church, Paul often with George Emmert in tow. During the Sunday School assembly at the Alliance church each Sunday, persons with a birthday would go forward to put in coins in a jar held by Walter Williams in an amount equal to their age. On Grandpa Pippert's last birthday, he went up and put in a penny for every one of his 76 years while they sang and sang the usual hymn:

> A happy birthday to you, a happy birthday to you; May you find Jesus near, every day of the year; A happy birthday to you, a happy birthday to you, And the best that you ever had.

One Sunday in the summer of 1942, Grandma and Grandpa came to dinner. The next day or so, Grandpa came over to help run the oats binder and he sat outside the house under a box elder tree and patched the canvas. A night or two later, an owl hooted outside Mother and Daddy's bedroom, and they remarked to each other: "There's going to be a death in the family." A day or two after that, the call came — Grandpa had had a heart attack. Daddy drove our gray 1940 Chevrolet in to see him, and after Daddy started home, the call came that Grandpa had died. When Daddy drove into the yard, Mother and we kids went out to tell him. Daddy's head snapped back at the word, and he turned around and drove back into town. It was not the only time he had to drive with the word of a death — the same happened when Chuck was killed while Daddy was appraising in Dyersville. He never said what his thoughts were on either of those drives…

But since that experience, I never hear an owl hoot without inwardly shivering — and we had a lot of owls on the farm.

One letter that Grandpa wrote in 1940 concluded: "I, like many others, am living on borrowed time; let us be prepared when the call comes to meet our Savior face to face." And when he did die less than two years later, his obituary noted: "He was converted fifty years ago… His life as a Christian and churchman was marked by the characteristics of daily reading of the Bible, regular attendance at worship, and generous contributions to both foreign and home missions."

Grandpa Pippert died relatively well-off. He had the acreage he lived on, a small farm near Clear Lake, and three houses in Mason city, all that property Daddy had negotiated with Allan Beck. Grandpa's will left the income from the property to Grandma, with the property going to his children after her death. As Daddy tells it, Grandma immediately 'broke the will' and moved to sell the property, even though the properties were left to the children. But the properties were sold at dirt-cheap prices (for instance, the three houses went for about $6,000 each, including one in posh Forest Park). The arrangement was for the money to go to the seven children, but they paid interest on it to keep Grandma going during the rest of her lifetime. Often Daddy and Uncle Calvin sat in Calvin's Plymouth out in the yard, presumably talking at length about the estate. When it was settled at last, I wondered, now what will they talk about?

Grandma moved into town, at 111 NE 7th St., the old Kew house, just around the corner from the Alliance Gospel Tabernacle. We generally would stop in after church on Sunday nights, and I would read the *Cub Gazette* in Saturday night's *Globe-Gazette,* which hadn't yet been delivered on rural routes. Getting to and from high school was a daily problem for me, since Mason City then had no buses and I was not old enough to drive. Perhaps a dozen times or so I stayed with Grandma. I would clear her walk with a damn small coal shovel; a couple of times I 'borrowed' 15 cents from her to go to the Y and watch Wednesday night basketball leagues. She would simply and devoutly pray and read scripture; I remember how she put her hand to her mouth, as she would do, and laughed over the biblical story of the pigs with demons in them leaping over a cliff. I saw that place on the east side of the Sea of Galilee decades later and thought of Grandma's laughter.

Daddy was always respectful in his relationship to his mother, and presumably, although I didn't really have a chance to observe this, to his father. Yet their slights must have hurt him, as when Grandma chose Uncle Calvin, and not Daddy who, after all, was the eldest, to be administrator of Grandpa's estate on grounds that Daddy was 'too busy'. I'm sure he interpreted this to mean, "Daddy's not as sharp as Calvin." Yet, it was Daddy who had salvaged the deal with Allan Beck. At the end, Daddy and his brothers and sisters each received $3,500 from their parent's estate. Daddy had received a $3,000 loan, which absorbed most of what he inherited. He pointed out that he paid interest on his loan all through the years, although not all of his brothers and sister paid interest on their loans or inheritances from their parents.

Mother's relationship was more adversarial to them, especially Grandma. I sensed in her a sort of grudging respect for Grandpa Pippert. She would quote him, "If you want to get along with your husband, keep his stomach full." Often, in later years, Grandma would say something hurtful to Mother, and Mother would dissolve in tears. Chuck and Marie, especially, resented this and more than once they bluntly told their grandmother, in effect, to stop being rude to their mother. Yet I always had the feeling that in these confrontations, as in most confrontations that Mother experienced, she won. The grandparents probably took a typical chauvinistic view toward the role of women, and Mother did not fit that subservient role at all.

The Uncles and Aunt Ruth

Calvin, the No. 2 child, was in all likelihood the person Daddy felt most comfortable with in all the world. They talked by the hours, sitting in Calvin's car out in the yard or standing by their machinery out in the fields. And he probably was the favorite uncle of most of us, certainly mine.

Uncle Calvin is lean, has a gold tooth, and is what the family called 'a jokester'. He always wore gray and white pin-stripe overalls (in contrast to all-blue overalls), with the top button on the side rakishly unbuttoned and tucked in. You could always tell how old Uncle Calvin is — he was born in 1900. He married Mabel Sandy, and they had two daughters, Naomi and Janice, born eighteen years apart. Naomi's first marriage to Ken Morphew, who was physically abusive, failed, and she later married John Sally and lived on the West Coast. Janice married Howard Cook and lives on the far north side of Chicago.

Uncle Calvin farmed a 120-acre place on both sides of the road just north of where old US 18 turned south, since 1969 the site of North Iowa Area Community College. He was especially proud of a row of black walnut trees and wrote into the contract they must not be uprooted. He also farmed 'the 80' just north of our farm which several of us brothers and sisters bought after Mother's death to make mile-long rows. Calvin was what Mother and Daddy used to call 'a money-maker'. He had an Allis-Chalmers tractor, and one of the first combines (also an AC) and four-row planters in the neighborhood. He also sold insurance and generally was here and there in the neighborhood, spinning about in his Plymouth. He was still driving at 89.

Ironically, both he and Uncle Arlyn sold their farms too early — and I believe it's entirely likely that Daddy surpassed them in wealth at the time of his death. They sold in the 1960s at $600-$800 an acre; Daddy's land was worth twice that amount when he died in 1976.

Once while I was in country school, Uncle Calvin asked me, jokingly of course, if I could help him that Saturday, and when Saturday came, Mother and Daddy had a hard time convincing me that he was only kidding. Calvin had a magical effect on Daddy. He hadn't wanted to go to the wedding of one of his grandchildren, but when Uncle Calvin offered to drive, he went with delight. The last week Daddy was alive, I was home for a few days. One evening, as usual, we made a trip to Clear Lake to see Uncle Calvin and Aunt Mabel. It was the last social visit Daddy made.

Uncle Earl, No. 3, born 1902, and Uncle Arlyn, No. 5, born 1910, were a world of difference from my father. Earl was profane, told tall tales, and was frankly often not nice to our immediate family. Arlyn, as Uncle Jess put it to me recently, "walked out of the family 40 years ago." He does zero to maintain any kind of contact with the rest of the family, although he seems to welcome their contacting with him. Of course, he always shows up for funerals — but no more than that. Neither he nor Earl returned to the church for the reception after Daddy's funeral.

Earl was a bit more swarthy than Uncle Calvin. He wore his hair combed straight back with small eyes, a bit like Lyndon B. Johnson. He married Clover Reynolds (1904-53) and they had three daughters, Irene, Jovetta, and Pat. As Paul tells the story, one time when Chuck came home from the Navy, the two of them went to a spot on Clear Lake's notorious east side — and lo! who should be in a nearby booth but their aunt Clover. When she noticed them, as Paul tells it, she carefully shielded her face with her hand to keep from being seen. Clover died at age 49, and a few months later, before the sheets were cold, so to speak, Uncle Earl married her cousin, Berniece, who was a boss in one of Mason City's dime stores.

Uncle Earl, who lived in a home in Central Heights given him by the grandfolks, was quite literally all over the lot — he worked in the shipyards in Vancouver during World War II; he helped build the Alcan Highway through Alaska and Canada; he drove a truck on runs into Chicago; he worked in construction. In fact, he helped build the concrete pit that houses the water pump on our farm, which Chuck paid for during World War II. The frame that Uncle Earl built to hold the wet cement started giving way and Earl had to hold it with his toe to keep it from collapsing. Check out that pit now — and you'll find the east wall bulges out at the bottom.

He told preposterous stories. I remember his telling about one run into Chicago. He was walking down the street when he felt himself being pickpocketed. He said he reached around, grabbed the kid's wrist and twisted, "and I heard it snap, just like chalk." Uncle Earl was not nice to either Chuck or Harold, a fact that hurt Daddy. I know that at least a couple of times, in the case of both Chuck and Harold, Daddy asked Earl in almost a plea: "Why do you treat that boy the way you do?" Of course he had no good answer. Uncle Earl died in 1988, and his funeral was the day before Vernon Dahl's, a gentle, soft-spoken friend of the family at the Alliance church. Uncle Jess summed it up to Harold and me on the way from the cemetery: "What a difference in the two funerals!"

His daughters did not seem to have the resentment toward other family members that Uncle Earl did. Irene was jovial; Pat was a feisty little girl who told me later that Chuck took her dancing. Irene's first husband, Robert Widdrington, was one of the first casualties from Mason City in World War II, in Alsace, France, December 13, 1942. She later married Dudley Mariner. Chuck was quite close over the years to Irene and Dudley. Dudley sold tires, I seem to recall. Jovetta (9/5/1925-1/25/1952) died too early of hypertension, nine years to the day before Chuck. Chuck sat up with her during her final nights. Pat, who acknowledges she was "the apple of my dad's eye," married a pilot, Jack Ward, in 1950 and lived in southern California and made a bundle off real estate.

Violet Ruth, 1908-1971, who went by her middle name, was the only daughter and had six brothers. She was easily the favorite of all. She was tall and lean, like Grandma Pippert, and had a friendly and gracious manner. She married Arthur C. Core, whom she met when they were students at the St. Paul Bible Institute. Their wedding date was two days after my birthday in May 1934. That fall, Lois lived with Aunt Ruth and Uncle Arthur in Browersville, Minnesota, in the Iron Range country, for her first year in high school. Lois and Aunt Ruth were close, and alike in build and manner, tall and gracious. Uncle Arthur went far beyond SPBI. He studied at Cambridge and got his Ph.D. from the University of Nebraska and held the chair in church history at Bonebrake Seminary in Dayton, Ohio, which later became United Seminary after the EUB merger in 1946.

Leslie and Jesse, 'the twins', although they did not look alike, brought up the rear. Uncle Les was graduated from the St. Paul Bible Institute, and Taylor University, the first in a list of three generations of Pipperts (including the Comstocks) to do so. Uncle Les held pastorates at Grantsburg, Wisconsin, where he met and married Violet Taylor, the daughter of a judge, Lyle, in Echo, Minnesota — Paul went there a time or two to work·in threshing rings — Aberdeen, South Dakota, and Hazel Park, Minnesota. His administrative ability was clearly recognized, for he became treasurer of SPBI, then treasurer of the C&MA Northwestern District, then district superintendent, and then Home Secretary, in charge of all domestic churches in the C&MA. He was hard-driving, sponsoring conferences in evangelism, encouraging construction of attractive new churches instead of the unsightly store-fronts typical of many Alliance churches, made evangelists who felt the Lord's call to hold conferences in Florida during the winter months, get off their duffs and start working. And he worked. He lived in Nyack and would commute to Alliance headquarters at 244 W 44th St. in Manhattan. If he got in late the night before, he would not sleep in but would head off to work at the usual time.

In a eulogy, Bernard King, also a national officer of the C&MA, wrote:

> If some would say that he worked too hard or drove himself too fast or was too impatient, no matter, Leslie Pippert was persuaded that God had given him certain responsibilities, and he was uncompromisingly faithful in his trust… If he drove others, it was because he drove himself. He was a man of action, and he expected others to act, too. But beneath a sometimes-autocratic exterior he was a man of God, a man who loved men, a man who loved the Savior, a man who served his Lord with heart, soul, mind and strength.

There was a gentle side of Uncle Les. I visited their home in Nyack overlooking the Hudson River, and he and Aunt Violet talked about children. Violet said that she and daughter Louise let babies cry for twenty minutes before picking them up. Uncle Les squirmed noticeably and said how he himself felt pain to hear a child cry. In later years, so it seemed to me, he and Daddy spent increasingly more time together, more time talking, more time at the farm. Uncle Les and Aunt Violet had two daughters — Marilyn, who always was frail, and Louise, who was husky and lusty. Marilyn died at 25 in 1961, the same year as Chuck and Grandma Pippert, and Louise died unexpectedly in 1979. By the time she was 66, Violet had lost her husband and both of her children. She spent her retirement in the Alliance home in Florida.

If Uncle Calvin was the favorite, Uncle Jess was not far behind. He was slight of build, did not marry until he was past 30, and before World War II was a teller at First National Bank, hence his brothers' nickname for him, 'The Banker'. Jess was the first person from the Alliance Gospel Tabernacle to enter the army during that war. He was stationed in Panama's Canal Zone for three years, and Grandpa's 1942 funeral was delayed a week to allow Jess time to get home. Two years later, after a long romance, he married Dorothy Young, a raven-haired young lady with a lovely voice at the Alliance church who always managed to communicate a bit of lasciviousness. Her singing of "Indian Love Call" seemed to be a staple at many weddings of our family and others at the church. I was a junior best man, and Carolyn Wagner, Dorothy's niece, was junior bride's maid, at the wedding.

After the war, Uncle Jess became a successful farmer near Osage and Aunt Dorothy taught. He was proud of his reputation as a farmer. In their retirement they moved to Northwood. Dorothy fought bad health, while Uncle Jess did everything — church morning and night on Sundays; the Masons; the Lions; bowling; trips here and there. He made a special trip to see Lois in Texas during her last illness. When Harriet was in Manly, they stopped by to see her weekly.

The Other Pipperts

While I was covering the White House, my Associated Press (AP) counterpart was Maureen Santini. One day one of the press staff came to me and said: "Did you see television last night?? It was the story of the Pipperts and the Santinis !!" It was the three-hour 1979 CBS movie *Orphan Train*, about trains that carried abandoned children from New York to Iowa. One of the featured children was Ben Pippert, carried west at age two and living in Dysart, Iowa, at 87 at the time of the film. Another was named Santini. During my time as a student at the University of Iowa, while driving between Mason City and Iowa city, I used to pass a big barn with 'Pippert' painted on it. It could well have been Dysart where I saw it; it was that general area.

According to an organization that was making up coats of arms, there were fewer than 300 households carrying the Pippert name in the United States (I think Paul and I must have heard from half of them…). While I was preparing for my 1964 trip, I checked the Chicago phone book and found three Pipperts (I no longer check phone books for Pipperts). One, Dr. Donald Pippert, I tried for three years to reach. The second was someone named Pierre Pippert (that French connection again). The third, John Pippert, comes from four generations of Pipperts in Amherst, Ohio. He was single, a physics consultant, and traveled a great deal, but seldom found any Pipperts, he told me. "But all the Pipperts I know are hard drinkers," he said. "I'm having a party. Want to come out?"

Mrs. Donald C. Thayer of Albany, N.Y., nee Sandra Ruth Pippert, wrote in 1980 that she had checked all the phone books in the United States, Canada, and Mexico (Mexico?? Can you imagine finding a Carlos Pippert? or a Fernando Pippert?) and had found only 24 Pipperts total. She was the daughter of George Henry Pippert, son of George William Pippert.

Arvilla Pippert Carroll, of Sacramento, Calif., wrote in 1979 that she married Henry William Pippert in 1927, had a son who graduated from Brigham Young University, and five grandchildren, all active Mormons. She said a genealogist had traced their ancestors to Niedermöllrich, but I wrote her I believe they were from the other strain of Pipperts there.

Martha Baldwin wrote from San Diego in 1959. Her mother was the sister of Henry Pippert, of St. Joseph, Missouri. Glenn Pippert, of Kansas City, son of Henry Pippert, moved from St. Joseph, Missouri, to Sacramento, and his wife and son were still living there. At the Library of Congress, I found a book in German by Elsa Bernhoffer-Pippert. The translation of the title (Täuferische Denkweisen und Lebensformen im Spiegel oberdeutscher Täuferverhöre) was *Baptismal Way of Thinking and Living in the Reflection of Upper German Baptismal Hearings*, or something like that.

And of course, Ruth Pippert Randol, of Nashville, where this long chapter began. Over the course of several letters in 1979, we gathered we might have a common ancestor in Conrad Pippert, who is Great-Grandpa Pippert's brother. But there turned out to be two Conrad Pipperts born about the same time in Niedermöllrich. But her Conrad Pippert did not come to America until 1883 and went to work for a paper mill in West Newton, Pennsylvania, 30 miles east of Pittsburgh. He married Augusta Zeigler. Their two sons, Fred, 1870-?, and Wilhelm, 'Willis', also worked in the paper mill, and Willis became general manager of the International Paper Co. in Rumsford Falls, Maine. Fred's daughter was Ruth Randol. Ruth told me her family were Episcopalians. One of her sons was a mathematician at the Graduate Center of New York and the other was a first vice president at the investment firm, Dillon and Co.

Wava got a call the other day from a Pippert from near Dysart who pronounced it, "Pee-pert." So who knows. Ultimately, a mystery.

What, then, are we to make of the Pippert side of the family? It is a mystery to me. There is tremendous talent in the Pipperts. It is a talent that manifests itself in a huge number of ways; see, for instance, the varied talents ranging from philosophy to mechanics, from basketball to music. There is, at the same time, an exterior that often seems gruff and abrupt, and sometimes, as in the case of a couple of the uncles, it was a gruffness that was internalized as well. At the same time, the Pipperts have as much gentleness at their core as anybody — anybody - - I ever have known. The Pipperts are classic, hard-driving Type As. They are achievers, yet not acquisitive. Their faith is strong, but their demeanor is not pious. Their speech is often halting, yet often bordering on the eloquent. They are proud, terribly proud, yet not pompous or arrogant. They are highly emotional, but not demonstrative. It all adds up to a complexity that I have never successfully figured out and have stopped trying. Billy summarized it well to me as we sat in their yard three weeks after Chuck's death: "I could predict his every response, but I never knew what motivated him."

Chapter 4

The Halsors

The Halsors were gentle and genteel. And I can't think of them without thinking of Grandpa Halsor. He died when I was 30. Yet amazingly, I saw him only three or four times in my life, the first time when I was past 21. Unquestionably he was about the most important person in Mother's life, rivalling if not surpassing Daddy. She spoke of him in terms that approached adoration; she praised his love for God, his love for his wife (Marie, not Martha). I am certain that much of the key to Mother's complexity — and she was very complex — was to be found in Grandpa Halsor. But not the entire family shared Mother's exalted view of him, not Lois, not Paul.

One problem with telling the story about our family is that we focus on the progenitors carrying our name. But by tracking only the family with our name, within one generation we are probing only one-fourth of our lineage. To be more complete in this exercise, we would have had to track equally the Pipperts, Pelzers, Halsors, and Strommens (and the Browns, Wohlenhauses, and Refviks). We know much, much less about the Halsors and especially the Strommens than we do the Pipperts and the Pelzers.

The Halsors were Norwegians. Great-grandfather Abraham Halsor (1838-?) was born in Norway and married Martha S. Refvik (8/5/1838-11/11/1915). He was a fisherman, so strong, as Mother quoted Grandpa Halsor as saying, that he could bite a nail in two and hold the ropes on his fishing boat with his teeth during a storm.

Berent Abraham Halsor during military training in Bergen, Norway

Uncle Alfred provided this clarifying note about the Halsors and Norwegian names:

> In Norway, children took the first name of their father and added 'son,' but were identified more accurately by mentioning the locality they came from. Therefore, when your great-grandfather [author's note: Uncle Al must have meant grandfather, not great-grandfather] entered Officer's Military School in Bergen, the name 'Halsor' was added to his original name of Berent Abrahamson for identification, and it became *officially* his name. 'Halsor' was the area in which he lived on the Island of Vogsa, across a stretch of water from Bergen, and about 20 miles north on the island. 'Halsor' had no stores and was no town, but just a group of families living there, like we have 'Hillcrest' and 'Willowbrook' sections. When the residents came to the U.S., all took the names of the various areas they lived in. So, there are other 'Halsors' in the U.S. but they are not blood relatives. Some live near Madison, Wisconsin. Berent came to the U.S. in 1891 at age 22. The Island of Vogsa, Nordfjord, Norway, was not very big, but had several areas where people lived. The town nearest 'Halsor' was called 'Rodberg'. They had to row across the water to the seaport of Bergen. Most of them were small fishermen and small acreage farmers.

Great-grandfather Abraham is buried in Elmwood Cemetery, Mason City, not far from his son, Berent, and his great-grandson, our brother Chuck. Abraham and Martha had six children: 1. Mons, 2. Berent, 3. Bertha, who married Harry Larson and lived in the Twin Cities; 4. Stine Berg (8/16/1872-1/30/1972), who lived in Cincinnati, and often came to Iowa to visit; 5. Amelia, who married August Rhode, and 6. Jacob A. Halsor (1881-8/1/1967), a furnace man with Currie-Van Ness Hardware in Mason City for years.

We know little about these families. Great-aunt Bertha was Pentecostal and spoke in tongues long before it became chic. Great-aunt Stine had two daughters, Mabel (?-1971) and Therese (1902-?), who had two children, Shirley Hanford, who married Myron Kline, and Richard Hanford, a bright young man who was crippled by polio. They once came to the farm. Richard, who must have been in his 20s, and I played cat and rat. Somehow, he let me beat him and he told me it was only the second or third time he had ever been defeated. The secret, of course, is to put your X in the middle square if your opponent has first move and marks a corner. Marking the middle square on second move always assures a deadlock. Richard later lived in Greece. Shirley's children were: Randy, 1952; Michael, 1953; Douglas, 1954; Nancy, 1961; and Kathy, 1969. Great-uncle Jake and Great-aunt Josie had several children — Nora and husband Hugh Strain celebrated their 50th wedding anniversary in Ventura, Iowa, in 1975; Melvin, a foreman at Decker's; Clarence; and Manita.

The record is silent about the Refviks. Grandpa Halsor (l/19/1869-1/16/1965), as Uncle Alfred noted, was born in Vogsad, Nordsfjord, near Bergen. He was a sailor in Norway and went to Officer's Military School, as Mother often pointed out. His erect bearing and neat attire attested to this. He came to America in 1891 when he was 22. Grandma Marie Strommen (11/22/1866-6/28/1899) was born at Strommen Sondfjord, one of eleven children, seven of whom grew to adulthood.

Grandpa Berent A. Halsor and Grandma Marie Strommen Halsor

Grandpa and Grandma Halsor were married on the Hendrickson farm near Hanlontown, Iowa, on January 13, 1893, and their children were Alma

Matilda (11/25/1893-10/12/1903); Magda Elise, our mother, born February 10, 1895, in Worth County near Hanlontown; Bella Marie (1896-1969); and Alfred Melvin (1898-1979).

Tragedy struck Grandpa Berent soon. In June 1899, Grandma Marie had an operation on their kitchen table, black erysipelas set in, and she died. She was 32. Grandpa was left with four tots. Mother was 4.

B.A. Halsor and four children after loss of his wife, Marie

I would say this was the most traumatic event of Mother's entire life. I have wondered many, many times what Grandma Marie looked like and what she was like, and whether these things would help explain some of Mother's drive and strength. Within a few years, Grandpa's eldest daughter, Alma, a deep Christian, died just before her tenth birthday. As Mother tells it, Alma saw a gold star on the wall one night, God's way of saying she would be called home soon. This left Mother as the eldest child, and as the years were to prove, she was a typical big sister.

The January after her death, the following notice appeared in the *Decorah Posten* in Norwegian:

> The announcement is hereby given to my dear relatives and friends that my dear beloved wife Marie Halsor born Matheson has succumbed in death at the age of 32 yrs, 7 months, 6 days. She was born in Strommen Sondfjord, Norway, November 22, 1866, and died June 28, 1899. The very highest was your love in life and very heavily missed in death. Very blessed be the remembrance of you. I with 4 small children mourn very heavily the remembrance of a beloved and faithful wife and mother. Berent A. Halsor.

Written across the bottom of the translation years later was the note, "My father did not know the American language very good at this time. Al H." Uncle Al did not recognize the simple eloquence of what his father had written.

In the 1970s, Mother got a couple of letters from her cousin Sophia A. Strommen, 1725 K St., Apt. 305, Sacramento, CA 95814, with a Bible verse seal on the back of the envelope. The letters provide what little we know about the Strommens. Although she did not state the relationships directly, her husband probably was Marie's brother. He was four years older than Marie. Sophia herself was one of eleven children, seven of whom grew to adulthood. Her eldest sister Alma lived in Sioux City, her sister Mabel in Gayville, South Dakota, her sister Audrey in Salt Lake City.

"My mother often talked about your mother, but it seemed that after she died that my parents lost track of the family," Sophia wrote my mother. "I remember my mother saying that your mother had visited my folks once. She had a baby girl with her. Wonder if that baby could have been you."

Berent and his brother Jacob Halsor. On the back of the picture is written: "The chain on locket my father is wearing is made from our mother's hair (Marie Strommen)." - Magda

At least eight of Grandma Marie's daughters, granddaughters, and great-granddaughters carry her name, including my own daughter, Elizabeth Marie.

As I recall from what Mother said, in the earliest years of his marriage Grandpa farmed.in what is now southeastern Mason City — if I were to guess I'd say on about Hampshire and 10th Streets. Mother says that as a young girl she remembers climbing to the top of the haymow and running into hornets. She leaped down the three tiers of bales to the ground floor in about three huge steps.

After Grandma Marie's death, Grandpa left the farm and moved to Mason City. He was a cabinet maker at the Mason City Millworks until his retirement in 1923, and as Uncle Alfred told it, it was he who invented the indented base of the kitchen cabinets and cupboards that is so widely used today. There he worked with Otto Dahl, later a stalwart at the Alliance church. He and his growing brood lived at 7th and S Federal; later, the house was moved to SW 4th Street just south of the Mercy Hospital and there it is to this day.

B.A. Halsor, age 88, November 1958

Every Sunday, Mother recalled many times, Grandpa would tuck his Bible under his arm and walk several blocks to Elmwood cemetery to visit Marie's burial site, a practice he presumably continued even after he married Martha. He also was a faithful participant at the Trinity Lutheran Church, then on SE 4th St., serving as Bible school superintendent and singing in the choir. A book called *The River*, mentions Berent's faithfulness at the church. He organized the Midland Heights Sunday School, now known as Our Savior's Lutheran Church in Mason City. Billy Sunday, the Chicago major-league baseball-player-turned-evangelist came to Mason City in the early years of the 1900s, and Grandpa got converted. Mother did under the ministry of N.K. Lorenson, leading her to quit as organist and Sunday School teacher at Trinity.

One of the enigmas of Grandpa's life was that he seemed to have an aversion to staying single. He married, and married, and married. Mother was a bit defensive about this but never offered a satisfactory explanation. On Nov. 28, 1900, about seventeen months after Marie's death, he married Martha Mellem (12/21/1864-3/15/1952) who also was born in Norway, and they had a daughter, Esther Carol (1901-1974). Grandma Halsor had three sisters, Mrs. Iver (Gunhild) Berg (2/3/1875-2/18/1958), Mrs. Mikkel Jorde, and Ole Larson, all of whom came to the United States, and a brother and a sister in Norway. Iver, who did some cabinet work for Mother's kitchen, died in 1953 and Gunhild died in 1958.

One measure of Mother's independence and strong will was what she called Grandma Halsor. Mother called her "Mamma," saying "She's not my mother." To us she was the only Grandma Halsor we knew. Then there were his California bride(s). But the wife with the most longevity was Martha. What kind of a marriage was it? How did she cotton to all those trips Berent made to Marie's grave? Why didn't Grandpa protect our mother from emotional abuse that Grandma Halsor apparently heaped on her and favoritism toward Esther ("He was Mr. Milquetoast," Lois remarked). What was the reason for the divorce?

In 1928, Grandpa Halsor moved to California because of poor health (did they divorce because Grandma Halsor didn't want to go?). He lived at 215 W Colorado in Montrovia, a suburb just to the east of Pasadena. After not seeing him for 18 years while she was raising her three youngest — and talking with him by telephone only once or twice — Mother, with Harriet and Harold in tow, took the train to California in the late 1940s to see him. "It was worth travelling 2,500 miles just to hear my father pray," she wrote me during a 1955 trip. "He still prays in the night as he used to."

In a California news clip, he attributed his longevity to shunning alcohol, tobacco and a third meal a day.

I was home in 1964 when Alfred brought him back from California on his first plane ride. Daddy, Shirley, and Carl went to the Ozark airliner to help with his wheelchair. It was quite poignant. Then we went to Auntie Esther's house. Grandpa was supposed to have been nearly blind for years. But around the table that night, Grandpa Halsor, at the head of the table, spontaneously offered grace, opened his eyes, and reached halfway across the table and speared a cookie. He had no trouble seeing that plate of goodies!

I used to kid that Grandpa went to California to die, but he finally died 30 years later of injuries suffered when he slipped off a step ladder putting up storm windows. Not quite accurate, but close. We laid him away on his 96th birthday, the oldest member of Trinity Lutheran church. Mother was serene.

The Halsors had great longevity. At death, Grandpa was 96; Aunt Stine, 99, Uncle Jake 86.

After the divorce, Grandma Halsor had moved in with Auntie Esther and Uncle Carl. Carl was something of a rascal, but to his credit, I never heard him make a slighting remark of any kind about his living arrangement at 1007 W State in the posh Forest Park neighborhood of Mason City. Heavy set, Grandma sat in an easy chair next to Auntie Esther's piano by the hour. "Think of it," she would utter whenever any of us grandchildren would say something. Or, as she sat down with something of a grunt and a plop, she would say, "Ufta," a treasured old Norwegian expression that Paul continues to use to this day. It probably bothered Esther a great deal that when death neared for Grandma Halsor, Mother, the stepdaughter, was the one she asked for, not Esther, the daughter. Because, unquestionably, Mother talked to her about God. She was buried in Elmwood Cemetery in Mason City, on the day Gordon was born, in a lot where Auntie Esther, Jerry, their good friend Gladys Elfstrand, are buried, only a few feet from where Chuck lies.

Halsors' 40th Anniversary, 1959: Esther Halsor Haase (half-sister, daughter to Martha Mellem), Bella Halsor Shields, Alfred Halsor, Magda Halsor Pippert

The Halsors and spouses: Bella and Shirley Shields; Esther and Carl Haase; Alfred Halsor; ?; Harry and Magda

Auntie Esther, in my opinion, was clearly the favorite aunt of us all. She was heavy set, belonged to Eastern Star and the Lutheran church (in that order), and baked superb cherry nut cake. Uncle Carl told jokes and flirted, was an accountant at Standard Oil, told jokes and flirted, belonged to the Masons, 32nd degree, and the Methodist church (in that order), told jokes and flirted. He once told a salesman's joke at a family reunion in which at the punch line he pulled down his zipper, yanked out his shirttail and said: "...and an Arrow for $2.98!!" Auntie Bella laughed. Uncle Shirley laughed, the smoke from his cigarette curling over his head. Daddy laughed, a bit embarrassed. Mother acted shocked.

Aunt Esther and Uncle Carl had only one child, a son, Jerry Lee (1/20/1937), who lived only hours. So she doted on her nephews and nieces, and indeed she did. She gave them piano lessons. She taught them about scrapbooks, a vice I have pursued with a vengeance to this day, and as I write this, I see six feet of my own personal scrapbooks on our shelves.

She took great pride in whatever we did. I could not have asked for more in an aunt. We sometimes would stop by on Sunday afternoon. Daddy always seemed a bit uncomfortable, although Aunt Esther and Uncle Carl unfailingly treated him with great cordiality.

Aunt Bella (4/10/1896-9/26/1969) was Mother's only full sister. She was married (2/10/1917) to Shirley W. Shields (1/14/1896-8/16/1975). They spent their years on farms in Worth County and Cerro Gordo County, except for seven years in California. They had two children, Harris Wendell (3/19/1918-5/14/1954) and Ernestine (8/2/1919-?).

Bella was an immaculate housekeeper. One could safely eat off her floor. For years they lived on a farm just east of Kensett, and every few months we would make the drive up through Plymouth to Highway 9, just east a few hundred yards over the bridge, and on north to their road. It seemed long and quite an event at the time, even though now it would be a bare 15-to-20-minute drive. Shirley, I guess, was a good farmer, but he gave it up, sold out, and moved to California soon after World War II. The relationship between Mother and Bella I would not characterize as intimate — close, for they were the only full sisters each other had, but not intimate. For one thing, Bella had been raised by another family and did not share Mother's high view of Grandpa Halsor. But probably more key was their difference over faith. Mother said that Bella had been converted when she was growing up, but 'threw it over' when Shirley told her he wanted no part of it. Which was surprising but maybe not, if you think about it — because Shirley's father was a minister. Bella loved Shirley, no question about that (Mother praised the quality of their marriage), so she threw it over. And Shirley smoked! I always remembered his smoking, the smoke swirling about his head, the smell of stale smoke in their house, those ashtrays-on-stands that they had. And later I guessed that Bella smoked too. She died in 1969, nearly fifteen years before her sister.

When she was 20, Ernestine married (12/27/1939) J.N. 'Junior' Methus, another farmer who soon left the farm and became a real estate man in Northwood. They had two daughters, Janice, and Marcia, who was lovely and devout. Harris had diabetes, so severely that he went blind in his twenties. He was an engineer for KGLO in Mason City at one point. He married Alma Brunsvold, also of Worth County, and they had two children, Serena and Jon. Harris' health went downhill and he died of diabetes at 36. And Harris' son Jon died in 1988 at about the same age, of a heart attack as he was working under his car. Marcia, who married William Young II, and Serena, who married Larry Holstad, a coach, especially were sweethearts and nice girls. In 1988, Serena's daughter was a band queen in the North Iowa Band Festival along with her third cousin, Heather, Harold's daughter.

Uncle Alfred (1/7/1898-4/26/1979) was the only son that Grandpa had, Mother's only brother, a banker, a fine man. He was tall, genial, hale. I wish I had known him better as a child. I had the feeling that as the years wore on, as often happens among brothers and sisters in advancing age, Mother and he grew closer. He began working at the First National Bank as a young man, and by the time he retired in 1963 after 46 years, he was a vice president. Someone once remarked to me that he was in line to be bank president. He didn't start smoking — cigars — until he was 40. After I finished college, I got three or four loans at First National. I would write Uncle Al, and within days there was the loan, totally unsecured.

He married Phyllis Letts (4/15/1898-9/29/1974), a regal woman of a good family in Mason City. They lived on E State Street in Mason City in a house that, to me, still looks like Phyllis! Later, in the 1940s and 1950s, they lived in a house on E State that may have been designed by Frank Lloyd Wright; at least, it certainly has the horizontal lines and long, overhanging roof that his houses did.

They had three children, Nancy Marie (2/11/1922-?), Richard Letts (6/20/1927-?), and Carol Mae (4/29/1932-?). Nancy was tall, with the same bearing of her mother and father. She worked at KGLO in Mason City. She married Parker Hession (2/8/1947), but he was killed a short time later in a car accident. She later moved to Colorado Springs and married Charles Freeman, an older man. They had a daughter, Candice Marie (born 10/29/1952), who skated well enough that she almost turned professional. Charles also died, leaving Nancy twice widowed. Richard married Jean Marie Moe (3/19/1928-?), daughter of a Mason City attorney and a beauty queen at Mason City High School. Their children were Richard, born 7/11/1952, Nancy Jean, 11/11/1957, Steven James, 10/4/1960, and Michael, 2/15/1964.

Carol (4/29/1932-?) was blonde and beautiful, Uncle Alfred's youngest. She was a grade ahead of me in high school, but it seemed to me that she moved in the social crowd a few cuts above my class. She dated Arthur 'Jack' Anderson (4/10/1931-?). He was short, blond, natty. Well! Within days after the 1950 high school graduation, they eloped. I remember Mother talking on the phone to Uncle Alfred when she learned about it. He was heartsick. Jack was Catholic. And, as it turned out, Carol was pregnant. Rose Marie was born Christmas Day that year. And the children came and kept coming — Andy, 6/7/1952; Martha Jo 4/28/1956; Mary Cathlene 4/12/1959; Teresa Jane 10/14/1960; Michael Ray 9/9/1961. Jack was in construction — his father had been with Pullman and later the Seabees. The growing brood moved and moved, and Jack made a lot of money. I got to know them when they lived in a northern suburb of Detroit in 1975-1976 while I was at the University of Michigan. They lived in a beautiful sprawling house and drove Cadillacs. They were very close to their children. Jack, a proud man, as it turned out, also was a gourmet cook. Carol preferred just to clean and keep a tidy house. Every night Carol and Jack went upstairs at 7 o'clock, their passion, apparently, still not spent. Becky and I and Jack and Carol went to Puerto Rico together in February 1981, soon after I had left the White House. Carol and I were amused. Becky also is a gourmet cook and she and Jack took turns trying to outdo the other as they alternated doing dinner. During those long evenings, Jack told stories — how he would go out to the machine shed to smoke when he was at our farm, how Aunt Phyllis would not let him bring beer into the house the first several years of their marriage.

When death came to the Halsor side of the family, it seemed to come in a bunch. Bella went first, in 1969. Auntie Esther and Auntie Phyllis and Uncle Shirley all died within 13 months in 1974-1975. Uncle Alfred died the very weekend in 1979 that Mother moved off the farm into the Manor, the old Hanford Hotel. It was a shame, because they would have been only a few blocks apart. Mother, the eldest child all of those years, lived another four years, the last survivor.

There are several reflections to make about the Halsors. As a family it did not seem to me that we were as close to them. To Auntie Esther, yes, but not to the others. I believe that Lois and Ernestine and Nancy and Chuck and Paul and Dick were much closer than Marie and Harold and I were to the younger cousins, just as on the Pippert side Chuck and Paul and Lois were much, much closer to Irene and Pat and Naomi than we younger ones were to Uncle Arlyn's son or Janice. And, despite the depth of Mother's religious belief, and that of Grandpa Halsor, too, if Mother is correct about that, the rest of the family did not seem to be especially religious. Uncle Alfred was active in the First Christian Church, but Aunt Esther was only nominally active at Trinity Lutheran. The cousins were not religious either, with a couple of exceptions — Nancy, who worked on a church staff in her later years in Colorado Springs; Marcia. But there was a quality and a graciousness about the Halsors that I always remember.

Harry and Magda, 50th wedding anniversary, 1970

Chapter 5

THE FOLKS

Mother and Daddy's marriage may have been made in heaven, but it certainly was not apparent during the first 30 years of their life together. But what was very apparent, to me, at least, was that the last 10 or 20 years of their 55-year marriage were golden, filled with as much joy and delight as any I have known. I think it was the fruit of persistence — divorce or separation never crossed their mind, I'm sure — as well as the fruit of clean living that didn't create unnecessary baggage or burdens. And they simply cared about each other and grew to enjoy each other's company.

MOTHER

When people ask about my mother, I generally say that she was one of the strongest women I have ever known, that she was one of the most devout Christians I have ever known, that she practiced what she preached (I never heard her lift her voice in anger, for instance, or rarely if ever did I see her lose her patience with the children), that she was quietly fearless, quietly determined, quietly effective. These currents converged into a flood that has washed over her family for generations. So much so that of her seven children and twenty-plus grandchildren, to my knowledge every single one is a believer, every single one is an achiever, every single one has a certain sweetness. This is all the more remarkable in a time of "shirtsleeves to shirtsleeves in three generations" where one generation makes it, the second generation exploits it, and the third generation squanders it. Like Daddy, Mother was honest to a fault. Like Daddy, hypocrisy and pretense were unknown to her. And in a time when everybody is insecure, Mother knew who she was. In a time of uncertainty, Mother was certain. My own children are vastly poorer for having not known her.

[I am a feminist, and by that I mean equal rights for women in every way. There are two women who are responsible for my position: Magda E. Pippert and Mabel Freligh. Both were strong, both very able, both gifted speakers. I didn't even know until after I left home that in the world, women were treated as inferior to men].

Over the course of her life Mother talked of her early years in three ways, and probably in this order — that she was "saved out of the Lutheran church" and became a Christian, that her father was heroic, and that her mother took up oil painting and turned Democrat. One of her paintings, a California desert scene, hangs in my office. She knew she was godly, but I think she had no inkling — to use one of her words — of her strength or her determination. On the other hand, I have a strong hunch that she knew how effective she was in getting what she went after whether it was something so minor as finding something that had been lost or misplaced, or so cosmic and eternal as praying her children into the kingdom and through their various crises.

Growing Up

Mother was born in Worth County, Iowa, on February 10, 1895, the second child of Berent and Marie Halsor. But her life was sent spinning early; her own mother died when Mother was 4 and her older sister died at 9 three years later.

What this meant was that Mother became the big sister in the family, and because Grandpa Halsor's subsequent remarriage was not satisfactory, she became the dearest woman in her father's life as well. Mother spoke often of the abuse she received from Grandma Halsor, her father's second wife; I am not sure what form the abuse took.

Magda Halsor, 1914

B. A. Halsor and second wife, Martha Mellem Halsor, with his 4 children by Marie Strommen, who died of 'black irrisyphilis' after baby Alma was born. 1906. Magda stands in front of her father. Magda later named her daughter, Marie, after Marie Strommen

The family lived on 7th and S Federal in Mason City. They attended the Trinity Lutheran Church, and Mother was baptized there and taught Sunday School and was the organist. One of her best friends was Helen Granholm. Mother worked as a maid for Charles MacNider, head of Mason City's wealthiest family, whose son Hanford became perhaps the highest-ranking non-career officer in the Army and General Douglas MacArthur's chief of staff in World War II. She says that it was there she learned how to 'set a table' and entertain; in later years, Mother did a lot of entertaining. Always there was a white linen tablecloth on her table, and it was set just right.

At Mason City High School, class of 1914 (her classmates included Earl Dean, Helen Granholm (later Diercks), Aurelia Krause, Prebe Thogerson, she took classes from Elizabeth Graves, as did Lois, Chuck, and Paul a generation later. She took a teacher-training "normal" course in high school under Fred D. Cram, later at Iowa State Teachers College (now the University of Northern Iowa) in Cedar Falls, that enabled her to begin teaching as soon as she graduated. She was very proud of having studied with Cram, who she said was a big, imposing man and very intelligent. She taught a total of seven years, starting first at Portland No. 2, 1914-1915, the same school Marie, I, Harriet, and Harold attended a generation later; Portland 3, which Daddy had attended, 1915-1916; the Portland school (No. 6), 1916-1919, when she met Daddy; Hanlontown, grades 4-6, 1919-1920; and Burchinal, grades 4-6, 1920-?, where she was teaching when she married Daddy.

Typically, Mother would take bed and board at the home of one of the school families, and then go back to Mason City for the weekend. At the Portland school, that meant riding the train between Portland and Mason City. She must have been something of a belle of the neighborhood, too, for she dated Glen McEachren and Elmer Krause, among others. She had pupils whose lives later were connected with ours through the years — like James Sandy, brother to Aunt Mabel and whose wife Norleda taught six of us seven children. After Mother was married a few years, she returned to education to serve as Deputy County Superintendent of Schools under Pearl Tanner, as nephew Gary points out, "ample evidence that her credentials must have been highly regarded." Mother frequently referred to her teaching and I am sure it helped shape the way she raised her own children.

But by far the most important experience in the early years was her conversion experience. At one point in her early years, she and her father went to a tent meeting held by Billy Sunday. Grandpa was saved. Later, under the ministry of an itinerant evangelist, N.K. Lorentzen, who never prepared a sermon but simply started preaching, she was saved. She soon felt that she should leave the Lutheran church and so informed G.K. Belsheim, the Trinity pastor who had confirmed her. He called her into his office and tried to dissuade her from leaving. "But when he went to pray, his words just sounded dead," she would say, "like they were bouncing off the ceiling. They didn't go any higher than that. But Brother Lorentzen. When *he* would pray, ohhh," she would say, raising her eyes skyward and clenching her fists. She took part in the Portland prayer meetings that she said later became the core of the Alliance church in Mason City.

Soon she felt the call to become a foreign missionary to Africa. She became the first Mason City member of the Christian and Missionary Alliance, which would send her to Africa without attending Bible school on the strength of her teaching experience. She raised her support and prepared to go. She told me many years later she was planning to go to Sudan. But she did not go. Marie has asked: "Why did she not go??" I confess that upon reflecting on it, I don't know the answer either. She would say to me, "I stayed and raised a family to become missionaries." And indeed, Lois served three terms in Colombia and Brazil; Harold made two short-term mission trips to Haiti; Marie married a minister; I was lay pastor for four years and married an evangelist; Harold's wife became a lay pastor; and among the grandchildren, Richard and Jay became ministers and Greg was a Campus crusade staffer.

Did Mother not go because she met Daddy?

AS MOTHER

To this day I remember as a boy when Mother would have been 'uptown' shopping. The afternoon would be nearing a close, and I would keep looking west to see if she was corning home. At some point, I would see a cloud of dust come flying past Hughes, the first neighbor to the west, go up over the slight hump 'at the corner', the first intersection a quarter of a mile west, and then the gray 1940 Chevy would turn into the yard, come

Harry and Magda Pippert, before the wedding, Nov. 4, 1920

to a braking halt, and out would step Mother, wearing that little straw hat and always a dress and stockings, under a burden of sacks of groceries and whatever.

She always was in a hurry. On Sunday mornings, Daddy would be in the car, dressed and waiting — and honking the horn. Mother was still inside scurrying around, trying to squeeze in one last thing before going off to Sunday School and church, sticking in the oven pot roast, potatoes, onions, and carrots to cook during church (a practice her daughter Marie follows to this day). We thus almost always arrived at Sunday School after the opening assembly had ended and classes begun. There certainly was no lassitude or laziness in Mother's being late, but it left an indelible impression on us, especially Paul, who vows he has never been late in his adult life.

And she worked. There was no sauntering around the house; always it was a fast walk. She used to say that her grandma had told her that as a child she never walked anywhere, always she ran. The houses where she and Daddy lived often had no closets, no running water, no electricity. Yet her house was always tidy, and she never went to bed with dirty dishes in the kitchen — ever. If company was coming, she would take the broom — the broom! — and sweep the yards.

Mother always had verses or little homilies hanging on the wall. Two stood out in my mind (and now hang in my kitchen):

>Only one Life-
>'Twill Soon Be Past,
>Only What's Done
>For Christ Will Last.

and

>*What God Hath Promised*
>God hath not promised skies always blue,
>Flower-strewn pathways
>all our lives through.
>God hath not promised
>sun without rain,
>Joy without sorrow,
>peace without pain.
>But God hath promised
>strength for the day,

Rest for the laborer,
light on the way;
Grace for the trial,
help from above.
Unfailing sympathy,
Undying love.

It never occurred to me while I was growing up that my parents were social. But now, as an urban dweller and suburbanite, I see how much more my parents entertained compared to people these days. Sunday dinner was always a special occasion in our house, and at least once a month we had company, almost always a family from church. Even more often, a family or a relative would 'drop in' unannounced on a Sunday afternoon or an evening. That, of course, is unthinkable in the city these days.

If it was Sunday dinner, Mother would have fried chicken and mashed potatoes and gravy and pie, most likely. Often it was rhubarb pie, made from rhubarb behind the house. And she would lead the song as they came to the table:

Come and dine, the Master calleth, come and dine;
You may feast at Jesus• table all the time,
He who fed the multitude, turned the water into wine,
To the hungry Jesus calleth — come and dine.

If people dropped in, Mother would 'visit' with them in the front room for an hour or so, then slip into the kitchen and 'stir up' a cake from scratch (no mixes) and make coffee. I remember the Pippert uncles — Calvin and Earl and the others — always would protest against having lunch. You would have thought there was something morally wrong or socially unconscionable about having lunch, but they always ate what she served. As Paul has said, "Mother made a pretty mean cup of coffee, you know." Her secret was to start with fresh cold water and later put an egg in to collect all the grounds, then scoop it out.

Her staple snack for the family for years and years was ginger creams, and I suspect she made not hundreds but thousands of pans of ginger creams. Generally, we ate our meals in the dining room around a round table, squeaky with wobbly legs. The meals I also remember vividly were in the screened-in back porch with a full view of the groves and flowers and the sound of the birds. Chuck and Pauly and I sat next to the wall, Lois and Marie opposite, with Daddy next to the outside door and Mother closer to the kitchen door. Harold was squeezed in between Mother and the girls; Harriet was in her own chair, unable to come to the table.

Magda Pippert, Chuck, Lois (March 1924)

For breakfast Mother often made pancakes, and, in those days of no ranges or microwaves, what a challenge she faced! Never using pancake mix, she fried the pancakes on the grill of the wood-burning cookstove, which would fire hot and cold in moments. Or the breakfast was cold cereal or oatmeal, which she had great difficulty forcing down the children, at least me. Of course, every noon meal (dinner) and every evening meal (supper) had meat and potatoes. My big problem with eastern cooking is that they don't eat potatoes.

One recipe endures: a recipe brought to gourmet perfection by Paul later and given the appellation "Pippert potatoes" by Paulette:

> —Fry a mess of bacon (I use Hormels or Oscar Mayer since that means the hogs probably came from the Midwest).
> —Slice some raw potatoes (Paul peels them so not a brown spot shows; I just rinse them under the faucet for the moment, then slice them with the skins on. Paul removes the bacon grease, wipes out the frying pan with a paper towel, and then fries the potatoes in butter; I keep the bacon grease and fry the potatoes in it).
> —Slice some raw onions and mix in.
> —Fry the potatoes and onions, mixing in the small bits of bacon and sharp cheddar cheese and occasional flakes of butter and lots of freshly milled pepper.

Her grandchildren remember drinking a special juice aid that Mother got at the old grocery store on Highway 18 and served in multi-colored metal glasses. Of course, the well water was always the favorite thirst quencher on 'the place'. Gary remembers riding the tractor one hot spring morning when his grandpa must have been cultivating. Grandma came out with lunch about 11:30 — a ham sandwich, coleslaw and Kool Aid for Gary and the same for Grandpa. But he had hot coffee to drink, which baffled Gary, the temperature being so warm.

Mother was involved in her neighborhood. She didn't belong to Social Hour, rather she belonged to the Portland WCTU. In later years, she was Portland president starting in 1959, and later the County WCTU president, starting in 1966, and a state delegate in the early 1970s. She saw it more as a time of spiritual fellowship than a battle against booze. At the Alliance church, after the children were raised, she taught the Ladies Bible Class and was president of the Missionary Prayer band for three years 1959-60-61. I went with her once, and even though I was well aware of Mother's strength, it still surprised me how she whipped the women through the business meeting, coming close to completely controlling it. Again, I don't think — although I'm not sure — that she ever had the slightest clue how effectively and dictatorially she ran it.

I sometimes have wondered what, nowadays, given a degree or perhaps a master's degree, Mother would have been able to accomplish in the marketplace. She drove until she was 77 when she was seriously injured in an accident in which a tail-gaiter croqueted her car as she had stopped to make a left turn into the drive. State Farm wouldn't settle. I took the case to two congressional lawyers, Jane Frank and Michael Pertschuk, later chairman of the Federal Trade Commission, who wrote State Farm. Even their clout didn't move State Farm. So Mother negotiated her own settlement with State Farm, and it was a good one, enough to buy Daddy a nearly new Chrysler that he proudly drove the rest of his days.

As busy as she was, there were two things that always took priority with Mother — her children and her faith. In retrospect, I think she disciplined more by dint of her personality and character than by the rod. I don't remember her ever lifting her voice in anger. Lowell Young recalled years later that, when he came to the home, he observed a well-disciplined family and Mother's utter determination. I don't think she imposed her will on any of the seven children in terms of their adult choices. In a day when parents dictate their children's choice of college and profession I went to high school and college where I wanted. Rather, the power of her influence in molding her children was in other ways. From the time we could remember, Mother led us children upstairs to bed, singing:

> March, march into bed;
> March, march into bed.

There, she would read Bible stories and sing songs and pray with each one of us.

> What a friend we have in Jesus,
> All our sins and griefs to bear!

> What a privilege to carry
> Everything to God in prayer!
> O what peace we often forfeit,
> O what needless pain we bear,
> All because we do not carry
> Everything to God in prayer!

The second verse begins:

> Have we trials and temptations?
> Is there trouble anywhere? ...

(Elizabeth and David sing that song every night, and when we get to the second verse, David's face invariably breaks into a broad grin that I can't discern is joy or mischief — or both.)

Mother pressed each one of us at her knee to make a decision to receive Jesus. Then, after we were asleep, she would go downstairs, and after the chores were done and the kitchen was clean, she would pray for us. She asked for, and got, a promise from God that He would save her children. She opened her Bible one night and the words leaped out at her:

> I will save thy children.

Mother could never say where in the Bible that verse was; she said God simply gave it to her. Years later, I found it: Isaiah 49:25. Every one of us knew that in any time of crisis, Mother was praying for us.

Her letters generally contained a spiritual note, a 'homily', if you will. "Remember — prayers are still going up to the throne of grace on your behalf. We're proud of you and may you always be a blessing to others for His glory," she wrote me as a college sophomore. In the last letter I received before graduating from Iowa in early 1955, she wrote: "We pray God's *very best* for you, for now, & the future. Keep looking up. With your eyes upon Him, every step will be right, & His will."

Her spiritual motto was "watch and pray." In 1953 when she was leading the Ladies Mission Band at church, their theme was "Intercessory Prayer — the greatest need of the hour." Often her place of daily — she never missed — Bible reading and prayer was out in the grove west of the house, early in the morning. Or she would pace the floors. During one crisis that one of her children was experiencing, she said she paced the floor in the dining room so much as to wear the carpet. In later years, her place of Bible-reading and prayer was her recliner chair. It now is in the room our nanny occupies, and I have told her that the chair has been immersed in as much prayer as any chair on earth.

Mother bragged about her children to other people. She may have injected too many spiritual points into too many conversations. It may have seemed too much at the time, but in retrospect, it was genuine without an ounce of pretense or pseudo-piety. It was real. She practiced what she preached.

Once she wrote me how she worked to keep back the tears whenever any of her children left home to return to school or work. "It's hard for me to part with my children," she wrote. "Outside of my Lord, *they are my treasure.*"

If Mother talked about her children and her faith a lot, she also talked about how hard she worked and the toll it took on her. Paul remembers her saying when he was a boy: "There will not be a mother in this home a year from now." In December 1946, Mother suffered the first of a string of heart attacks. It was early evening, and she had just run the vacuum and laid down. She said to call Dr. Henley, and he came and diagnosed a heart attack. I'll never forget that night, when we did not expect to keep her. I heard a Colgate dental cream ad on the radio during those long hours and it kept going through my mind; I never hear it to this day but what I don't think of that night. Chuck, now home from the Navy, sent Paul a wire and Paul came home from the army for a few days. Norleda Sandy came by to visit a day or two later and said she did not expect to see Mother ever up again. We also had called Rev. Young, and that night, as he did on a score of nights over the next several years, he came out, prayed and quoted verses through the night hours. It always had a healing effect. One of the chapters that Mother clung to was Psalm 103:

> Bless the Lord, o my soul:
> And all that is within me, bless his holy name.
>
> Who forgiveth all thine iniquities:
> Who healeth all thy disease.

When Mother died nearly 40 years later on April 8, 1983, it was her heart that refused to give up even days after most of her other vital signs had failed. Her heart really had been healed so that it was better than new.

She died in the arms of her youngest born with three generations in the room. Her funeral was held in the Alliance church — a denomination she had joined 65 years earlier as an aspiring missionary, and the sanctuary was packed upstairs and down. Her children and grandchildren stepped forward to praise her. And as Lowell Young, who had prayed those nights at her sickbed 35 years earlier, preached her funeral oration, tears ran down his cheeks. Her granddaughter-in-law Karen and daughter-in-law Sandy sang in Norwegian what had been Mother's favorite hymn:

Den store Hvide Flor...
(Behold the Host arrayed in White)

Daddy

Any time I start to feel the slightest bit smug about what I have done as an adult, I think of my father — where I started from, what I accomplished, the compromises I made along the way, and where he started from, the baggage he had to carry, the utter decency with which he lived his life, and what he accomplished — and I feel my pride shrivel. There simply is no comparison.

There was a Lincolnesque quality to Daddy — he suffered setback after setback after setback along the way, most of them not his doing, and yet, when he died he had achieved riches and gold both in his character and in his possessions. I never heard him tell an off-color joke in his life or use profanity; I'm sure the only woman he ever desired in his life was his wife; liquor or tobacco never touched his lips; to him, swearing was saying "Doggone it!"

The worst sobriquet he ever gave a person was to call-him "a cur." Daddy was a big man. He stood right at 6 feet, and the tall lanky man Mother married had added·a 100 pounds by the time we children were growing up. Mother thought his strength was prodigious, and it may have been. Once he picked up all seven of us children at the same time. Twice he had farm accidents that clipped off the tip of his right index finger, and the big finger on his left hand was permanently bent — something I copy to this day by putting my hand flat on something with my middle finger bent. He always wore pin-striped bib-overalls (the better to fit his bulging frame); I don't think I ever saw him in a pair of denims. He loved to have us children comb his hair with that wire brush and in later years he would ask me to tie his tie with a Windsor knot. He loved corn on the cob and fruit with thick cream, and, in general, Mother's cooking. And he always drank tea at night. He slept with one leg hanging out from under the covers, and when we kids would get the rare chance to peek, we used to giggle as he slept wiggling his toes.

Harry Vernette Pippert, 1898

Two weeks before he died, I left the Carter campaign trail and flew to Waterloo. He and Mother met me, and as we did so often, we drove, with Daddy at the wheel as always, the back trails to Mason City, with Daddy spinning tale after tale and stopping for coffee along the way. The moments were golden, so unlike many he had known in earlier years. The talk turned to the farm. "You're sitting on a gold mine," I told him. "I know it," he said.

It was one of the first times in my life I had ever heard him talk about his farm in terms other than a fear that he would lose it. He said it without an inch of pride or boast. We all know now that his estate was one of the most complicated that Morris E. Laird — and more about this kingly man in a moment — had ever handled. But that is not the point. The point is that in Daddy's mind, he was sitting on a gold mine. It was the gift of a thought that few people ever deserved having as much as he did, and I suspect it was God's way of pronouncing a benediction on a life that had been lived, not without adversity, but without compromise.

As for Morris E. Laird, he is accepted by bench and bar and people alike as Mason City's best lawyer. His office overlooks Central Park and Federal Avenue. Daddy had known him over the years and would speak of him in terms of great respect, and when Daddy died, it was natural we would seek out Laird. Laird became God's gift to us, another benefit of Daddy's well-lived life. If Daddy had tough knocks, Laird was the unchallenged best and he always won. He saved our estate, and he did it with skill, finesse, aplomb, and we had utter confidence in him.

GROWING UP

Daddy was the eldest of seven children of Charley and Emma Pippert. He was born September 23, 1897, in the same house in which he was living when he died October 21, 1976, a month into his 80th year.

I simply cannot forgive or forget the way he was raised. Daddy was the eldest and had to drop out of school after the eighth grade to work. His youngest brother and sister went to college. That simply is too much spread, too much favoritism in one family. It didn't get better. When Grandpa Pippert died, Grandma Pippert passed over Daddy and selected the No. 2 son, Calvin, to be administrator of the estate on grounds he had more time. But the blatant implication was that Calvin had "a better business head." Even though Daddy had salvaged the family fortune in a deal with Allan Beck (the problem is, of course, that we don't know what baggage Grandpa and Grandma carried from *their* childhoods). Daddy was born, as were several if not all of his six brothers and sisters, on the Old J.H. Pippert Farm, and it was the farm he later bought and lived on almost all of the last half of his life.

Mother told the story of when Daddy was a child, he needed new shoes. Rather than have him leave the field to get them, his mother bought some herself and brought them to him. They didn't fit, but no matter, he had to wear them anyway. Daddy went to country school at Portland No. 3, where Mother taught later, and still later the site of the KSMN transmitter, and his teachers included Gertrude McLeod Bauer and Maude currier Emmert who became his neighbors during their adult lives. I have no idea what discussion went on between Grandpa and Grandma as to whether Daddy should go to high school, but he didn't. And starting with Calvin, the No. 2 child, his brothers and sister all did, and Ruth and Les went to college.

Daddy did get to enroll for a while at the Hamilton School of Business in Mason City, and he said later that in his course there he learned his somewhat distinctive handwriting and some bookkeeping. His ability with figures was a source of pride to him throughout his life, and he enjoyed being on the audit committee at the Alliance Church nearly every year and eventually becoming township assessor. Daddy was the right age to have been drafted during World War I, but he said that he did not have to go because of the flu epidemic. Years later, he was just barely under the wire to register for the draft during World War II, and of course, at that age he did not go.

In 1919, when he was 21, he spent some time harvesting wheat in Canada near Winnipeg. This must have been quite a trek for a young man in those days; I think now that it revealed a streak of wanderlust in Daddy that was manifested later in his going west to California in the 1920s and traveling throughout Iowa and parts of Nebraska and Michigan as an appraiser in the 1950s and 1960s. This was the enigma: it was always hard to get Daddy to go on a family outing; yet I know he loved to travel.

Life was difficult for Daddy during much of his life. It seemed that tough luck never abandoned him. After he married, he moved from one farm to another as a tenant farmer; he didn't buy the home place — the same one on which he was born, until he was past 40. He and Mother moved to California in the 1920s, but their relatives followed them, their house burned down and he lost his crop of peppers. So, they moved back to Iowa. Always of generous heart, he lent $100 to a scofflaw named Swartwood which would be like $1,000 nowadays — and of course it was never repaid. In the east side of the barn on the home place in the 1940s, he built another row of stanchions — "stanchels," I called them — and bought a herd of Holstein cows from Giles Fry; within weeks they were diagnosed as having mastitis and he had to sell them for slaughter. In 1946 or 1947, he planted sugar beets as a cash crop; but the sugar beet factory in Mason City got Mexicans so late in the season that only a few rows could be thinned out. Harriet's long siege of rheumatic fever was punctuated by long stays in the hospital, and on at least one occasion, Daddy got his check from the Portland elevator for his season's crop of soybeans, took it to Mason City, and handed over the whole thing to Park Hospital.

Here was a man, not formally well educated, probably a battered self-esteem from childhood, beset by unremitting tough luck — and also

Magda, Harry, Paul, Chuck, and Lois, Nov 1925

married to a strong woman of strong determination and equally strong-willed sons who took it upon ourselves — though never Harold — to tell him occasionally what was wrong with him. Daddy's was a mountain-sized burden. He worked so hard as a boy that he never learned how to play. Only a couple of times did he ever try to kick a football that I might have been playing with. I remember that he once told me during spring work that, after the crops were in, we'd go fishing. But we didn't. He went to a basketball game only once or twice with the older boys; on one of those times, he said the evening was spoiled because upon returning home he had run over Harold's sled with the car.

Yet, there were flashes of light, hints of what might have been. I never thought of my father as being especially au courant on the matter of news; yet I would see him nightly reading the *Globe-Gazette,* far more than a lot of modern men read the newspaper. I never thought of him as being a sports buff; yet he always knew and talked about who was Iowa's football opponent that Saturday, whether Minnesota or someone else, more so than I am doing at his age then, and I am an alum.

Yet the biggest hint of what might have been was in his acumen uncovered at Hamilton's. Through the years he was an officer of the rural telephone company (our number was 22F21, meaning line 22 and the ring was two longs and a short), he was president of Portland No. 2 Independent School Board until — Harold finishing the eighth grade there — the folks let it be closed. He was township assessor for Falls and Portland township for years.

The best thing that happened to him professionally was related to this. In September 1948 he answered an ad in the *Globe-Gazette* for an appraiser for the J.M. Cleminshaw Appraisal Co., of Cleveland, Ohio. He was hired. Over the next 20 years he went to thousands of farms, measuring the buildings and appraising the value of the land and farmstead. I have a map of Iowa showing the county and the year: Cerro Gordo (Mason City) 1948, 1963-1964; Black Hawk (Waterloo) 1949; Dubuque 1960-1961; Johnson (Iowa City) 1962; Worth (Northwood) 1963-1964; Hancock (Garner) 1964; Lee (Keokuk) 1964; Franklin (Hampton) 1965; Sioux (Orange City) 1965; Humboldt 1966; Webster (Fort Dodge) 1966-1967; Wright (Clarion) 1969; Iowa (Marengo) 1969. This does not include his time in Nebraska city in 1952-1953, or in St. Joseph, Michigan, in 1961-1962.

What this meant, of course, was that Harold took over the bulk of running the farm at the ripe age of eight...And when Harold married in the 1960s and moved away from home, Mother, now in her 70s, stayed at home alone on the farm.

There was much that was basically bashful about Daddy; yet, given the right conditions, he loved to talk. He was capable of transcendent eloquence. He was one of the best raconteurs I have ever heard. He would come in from the fields in harvest time in the afternoons to sip coffee and talk. When Lois came home, often when Mother was in the hospital for one malady or another, Lois remembers that Daddy would keep her up until the wee hours, talking and recounting stories of yore. When Uncle Calvin would come over, they would sit in his car and 'visit' for what seemed like hours, who knows about what. When salesmen would come, Daddy often would engage them in long conversation. Some of those times, he would call to me to come over, and I knew what he wanted. He wanted me to show them my hand; I didn't mind in the slightest. He loved his assessing and appraising, in part because he loved to talk. He seemed to me much more at ease if he were alone, or at least not with people around from whom he felt an expectation to do it in a certain way.

One thing that characterized Daddy was his handling of gifts. Daddy always gave Mother big, unlikely gifts. When she was recovering from her heart attack in December 1946, he got her a Maytag gas range to replace the wood cook stove. I knew in advance what the present was going to be, of course, but I whispered loudly in Mother's hearing, "fur coat!" and that's what Mother expected. Frequently Daddy would go to Mason City and buy Mother a dress at Lundberg's on East State Street; invariably, it was an expensive one of good taste. But it was hard for Daddy to receive. He often would ignore what was given to him; in fact, he often seemed ungrateful. I think rather he just didn't know how to act. Mother gave him a handsome rocker in the later years; he seemed almost unhappy about it and rarely sat in it.

Daddy frequently had trouble with one eye. He would develop an ulcer on it. The first time, Dr. C.C. Chenoweth in Mason City treated him by giving him increasingly heavy doses of arsenic, then gradually reducing it. It worked. As the ulcers came every couple of years, it led to a life-long relationship with Chenoweth and his partner, H.D. Fallows, and their successor, Dr. John Dixon. They, too, are the only eye doctors I have ever gone to.

I remember yet the pride Daddy had. He seemed proud to be asked to be a pallbearer, as he was for Frank Emmert, Elmer Krause, and others. He was so proud of his job as appraiser. He got a cream-colored 1946 Dodge when he first began appraising, and he mounted his 10-foot measuring pole on top. He would drive into the yard after having been away all week, and get out, fairly bursting with pride. He had always loved Dodges, and he stuck with them hence. When I was a student at the University of Iowa in the early 1950s, he was appraising in Keokuk, and he came to see me on a Sunday morning. He was all dressed up, shaved, and lotioned. Often, he would take off months at a time, but as soon as Cleminshaw would call, Daddy would go back to work.

Yet even the Cleminshaw years ended in ashes. Daddy had slipped, fallen, and hurt his back on the job in, I guess, Marengo, and by this time, of course, he was past 70. After a few weeks, he went back to work only to have his supervisor greet him by laying him off. So he made the sad trip back to Mason City, all alone. He had worked for Cleminshaw twenty years and the sons of bitches of big business fired him.

Throughout much of his adult life Daddy often seemed over-burdened by waves of discouragement that manifested itself in an 'ornery' form when he clashed with Mother's quiet steel. If Mother wanted to go somewhere that involved some travel, it seemed that Daddy was sure not to want to go. That is, unless Uncle Calvin went. Daddy resisted going to Indiana in 1967 for Bart's wedding, but when Calvin offered to go, Daddy become enthusiastic. We would say, "Daddy is having a spell," but that is far too simplistic, I think.

Actually, at his core, Daddy was a gentle man easily given to emotion. After Grandma Pippert died, Daddy wrote his brothers and sisters from St. Joseph, Michigan, where he was appraising:

> I'm sure these parents of ours did what they thought best. They were common people who tried to teach us right from wrong, to be honest peaceable children. We were all taken to Sunday School without fail, to respect the rights of others, and as Mother wished, that we should be an unbroken circle on the other side.

More than once I saw his eyes well at something that would not move most people. My senior summer in college I sang in a quartet. A woman Daddy met told him how moved she had been to hear it. When he related this to Mother, his eyes filled with tears. I have seen him weep, sometimes in what apparently was despair or self-loathing after an encounter with Mother, sometimes over something like an encounter with C.D. Tieszen, the tough Russian who dictatorially pastored the Alliance church for so long. Mona Young, wife of the beloved pastor Lowell Young, suffered from migraine headaches. She told me years later that once, while she was having a headache, she had seen Mother and Daddy. Mrs. Young said that upon learning about her headache, Daddy's face took on anguish. He was perceptive. Wava first pointed this out to me, and I began to see that he probably was as perceptive in his judgment of character as anybody I have ever known. Mother was sensitive and caring, but Daddy was the one who was perceptive. He could catch the slightest nuance in a room. He was a superb test of character, and what made it so bad when he made a judgment about somebody, he generally proved to be right.

He was a great storyteller, but only if he got started spontaneously, for he would refuse to tell a story upon being asked to do so. The stories were not jokes, but riveting anecdotes about growing up or dealing with the neighborhood. For instance: Daddy said that he was riding a horse on old US 18 as a boy when he saw a figure all in black appear in the distance on the same road and it started coming toward him. The closer the figure in black came the more nervous Daddy's horse got, and as they passed, the steed reared. Later, Daddy found out that at the very moment he saw the dark figure appear down the road, someone had died at that place…

There was not an ounce of pretense in Daddy. I have often said that to my father, pretense was a worse crime than thievery. It affects me to this day, for I have a great intolerance for people who are showy or put on the dog or cut corners. He always deferred to others, even at home. If he wanted to say something to the preacher after the service, he would wait until everyone else had passed through rather than tie up the preacher in conversation while others waited in line. If one of the children called home, he invariably would quickly put Mother on. But if Mother happened to be away, or was in the hospital, I would have a really fine talk with Daddy, and found him interesting, gracious. I loved his telephone voice.

He knew the Mason City countryside and loved it. Some of the happiest times I have ever known were when I would go home, and he and Mother got in the front seat of the Chrysler, and I in the back, and Daddy drove miles and miles through the neighborhood — not just a few minutes, but through Rock Falls, Nora Springs, Rockford, Rockwell, Portland. He knew every neighbor, every road, every farm — and he had a story about each one. Once we searched out where the Willow and Lime creeks join south of Rockwell. Just before he died, we found where the Cedar and Shell Rock join north of Waterloo.

And he loved God. His Bible was worn — he always wrote in the margin alongside the text the name of the minister and the date. He used to remark to Mother that he didn't think he would die or that we children would grow to adulthood — for the Lord would come first. His *Daily Light* was as well-worn as Mother's. Psalm 91 was his favorite. One Sunday night at the Alliance church, the pastor asked for favorite songs. Daddy asked for No. 393, which was sung at Grandpa Pippert's funeral:

> Some day the silver cord will break,
> And I no more as now shall sing,
> But, o, the joy when I shall wake
> Within the palace of the King!
> And I shall see Him face to face,
> And tell the story — saved by grace:

The following is from Mother's 1967 Christmas letter:

> Last winter, after persistent hoarseness in Harry's throat, he went to the doctor. In days he was in Mayo Clinic. On a bitterly cold January morning, Harry's Bible lay open in his room at Rochester Methodist Hospital, and the children and I were there as he was wheeled away to surgery. A half hour later, Dr. Lillie, a wonderful man and one of Mayo's best, came to tell us Harry had suffered cardiac arrest and privately he told the boys their father probably was gone. We were stunned. But this did not take into consideration the bank of prayer which had been built up literally across the country for Harry. Three times that morning his heart was restarted though his rib cage was broken in the process. Dr. Lillie said it took a power greater than his to bring Harry back to life. He spent a week in intensive care under the care of a battery of nurses and doctors, one of them President Johnson's anesthesiologist (Dr. Didier). A few days later Harry started daily cobalt treatment for cancer on both sides of his vocal cord. In May, he was pronounced completely healed.

The morning Daddy had cardiac arrest was the same morning in January 1967 that the three astronauts burned to death. Paul, who was there, called Lois to say: "I think we're losing Dad." Daddy would go back to Mayo's every three months for an examination from Dr. Lillie, and you could tell that, as that time approached, he grew tense. But the healing had been complete.

Death came in October 1976, once again from cardiac arrest, this time at Park Hospital after he grew dizzy and unable to drive very well. I had been home ten days earlier and he and Mother and I had gone driving through the countryside, and on that Friday night we had gone to see Calvin and Mabel. It was, appropriately, his last social call. Harold was combining corn, and Daddy would grab a hold of the ladder on Harold's combine as it moved through the field, crawl up and stick his head in the cab to see how things were going. He crawled up on the wagon and ran corn through that big, thick hand of his to test the quality and moisture. I had returned to the campaign trail in New York at the Waldorf-Astoria for the Carter-Ford Al Smith debate when I called home and got the word that he was dead. By the time we went to bed that night, most of us were back in Mason City.

The funeral was on Sunday afternoon at the Hanford church where he and Mother had been attending. It, too, was packed upstairs and down. We sang his favorite hymns:

> Great is Thy faithfulness, O God my Father,
> There is no shadow of turning with Thee;
> Thou changest not, Thy compassions they fail not;
> As thou has been Thou forever wilt be.
> Summer and winter, and springtime and harvest,
> Sun, moon and stars in their courses above,
> Join with all nature in manifold witness
> To Thy great faithfulness, mercy and love.
> Great is Thy faithfulness! Great is Thy faithfulness!
> Morning by morning new mercies I see:
> All I have needed Thy hand hath provided
> Great is Thy faithfulness, Lord unto me.

The young minister preached. Toward the end of his sermon, he turned to us children and told us how proud Daddy was of us. It should have been the other way around. Then he turned to the congregation and told them that after the service a few Sundays before, he saw Daddy waiting off to one side while the others passed through the line to shake hands. When Daddy came over to speak, the minister said, he requested that sometime soon they have a service of rededication. Then the minister told the congregation: "He has passed on before we could have that service. We're going to close the service now by singing 'Amazing Grace,' and those of you who would like to rededicate their lives as a memorial to Harry Pippert, stand while we sing."

The entire congregation stood. All those neighbors, up and down every road that Daddy knew so well, who knew him by the quality of his life, every single one of them stood…

Mother and Daddy

Mother and Daddy met while she was teaching one of the schools in Portland Township, probably Portland 6. I am not sure exactly how they met, how quickly Daddy asked Mother out, how quickly they fell in love. Mother had dated at least a couple of men — Elmer Krause and Glen McEachran. Daddy, I suspect, had not dated before. What was there that drew this city-bred schoolteacher to this hardworking farmhand? Years later, Mother told me: "I could see what was there beneath that exterior." There are photos of the happy couple before their marriage, and poems that Mother wrote to him. I found some love letters between the two in an old radio in the shop at the farm, but they have disappeared. Here is one poem:

In remembrance of my sweetheart, Sunday, May 20, 1920

> The rippling stream went flowing by,
> The wind was softly blowing, The golden sunset in the west, Its crimson splendors throwing
> Its radiant rays of golden light, Upon a beautiful form was throwing.
> A ray of light as from heaven it came,
> To lighten an inward soul of God, so blessed, And find at Nature's door a resting place.
> May all Nature declare, Thy wondrous works, A finished product of an Almighty Hand!
> May thy soul, oh heart of God, so blessed,
> Declare the finished work of God in man!

And so they married on Thursday, November 4, 1920. Great-Grandpa Pippert performed the ceremony at Grandpa Tialsor's house at 701 S Federal

Harry and Magda Pippert, wedding day, Nov. 4, 1920

Avenue in Mason City, and Uncle Calvin and Aunt Esther were the attendants. All four were present at Mother and Daddy's 50th anniversary. A newspaper clipping described Mother as "a charming young lady" and Daddy as "a worthy young man."

> At 4 o'clock the bridal couple and attendants came down the stairway to the strains of Lohengrin's Bridal March, played by Miss Esther Tillotson, and took their places under a canopy of pink and white streamers. The bride wore a lovely traveling gown of brown broadcloth and carried a bouquet of pink roses. Following the ceremony a five-course wedding dinner was served to relatives of the happy couple. The color scheme of pink and white was carried out in the decorations and menu. Miss Mable Sandy and Miss Esther Tillotson assisted in serving the dinner.

[The 4 o'clock hour became something of a tradition. Lois, Marie and I all began our ceremonies at that time.] Mother and Daddy honeymooned for a weekend in Des Moines where Mother had to go for a teacher's convention. She was, I believe, teaching in Burchinal at the time.

It was apparent from the beginning that the marriage wouldn't be easy. Mother said Daddy had agreed to go to St. Paul Bible Institute — "for the next three months," the clipping said — but if they went, they were there only a few days. They stayed with Grandma and Grandpa Pippert for a while, and Mother says Grandma knocked on their door every morning at 7 and said, "Time to get up." Their first home was in what had been a chicken coop. I suspect all of these things were hard for a young woman whose own father was very gentle, who had been raised in a house that was as well-done as one might expect a cabinet maker's to be. Later I used to chuckle a bit upon thinking what a handful Grandma Pippert must have found her incredibly strong new daughter-in-law to be, compared to, say, some of her other daughters-in-law.

Thirteen months later, Lois Elise was born. Like all of the other children except Chuck, she was born at home, then a stone house near Taylor Bridge in what is now owned by the people who run a greenhouse.

The Golden Years

We leap ahead now to Mother and Daddy's last years, holding the family's "life together" for the final chapter.

[First, a few difficult words. The "life together" was not always golden. Daddy had 'moods' that seemed to come in waves, and Mother usually responded in tears. We children tended to hold Daddy responsible and to acquit Mother. What opened my eyes was a course, Psychology of Family Relations, which I took at the University of Iowa in 1954 as a 20-year-old senior. I had to write two Family Logs, and I wrote everything I could think of including the kitchen sink and the psychologist-instructor went over it with me. The main insight I gained from the course was: Mother had innate strength, but it was laced by a self-described modesty and a difficulty in admitting fault. I remarked in the log about Mother's "lack of a basic understanding of my father." In addition, "I think that we children have often been the biggest source of dissension between my parents," I wrote. "My Mother inevitably will take the side of us children no matter if she agrees or not. This happening repeatedly has often caused my father to feel as if he's 'always wrong and never right.'" As for Daddy, given his own crushed childhood, his often-unattractive responses to his high-powered wife and sons were quite predictable and understandable. "My father needs much encouragement," I wrote in the log. "He needs to feel wanted and needed." What he needed was affection and affirmation — given subtly, not obviously — and lots of it. I vowed after one occasion that never again would I ever confront my father. I shared some of these insights with my brothers and sisters. The Younger Four, I think, understood the dynamics better than the Older Three.]

I know now that there were cultural factors looming as well. Daddy was raised in a Germanic tradition of male dominance (curious, I once asked Paul who ran Grandpa and Grandma Pippert's household. "The Chief," he said without hesitation). Mother came out of a Norwegian culture in which women are strong and assume leadership (Norway, for instance, recently had a woman prime minister).

Should Mother and Daddy have achieved more materially? They bought the home place for $13,600 in 1938, about $85 an acre. Over the years nearly every place surrounding the home farm came up for sale. Daddy bought none. Paul feels, probably correctly, that we probably should have owned the entire section by the time Daddy died. The 110 (acres) on old US 18 adjoining the Ladwig place— which was farmed for so many years by Daddy — was purchased by Uncle Les in 1954 for $26,000, about $236 an acre, with $2,600 down and a $1,000 a year. When Harold and others of us bought the north '80' (acres) adjoining the home place in 1983, we paid $190,000, or $2,375 an acre. On the other hand, those were days of no insurance and more than once Harriet's illness wiped out a crop. That, and the bad luck, have already been detailed here.

But for all this, Mother and Daddy did things right. I have a theory that the real test of a couple is how their grandchildren — not merely their children — turn out, for their children will raise *their* children the way they were raised. And how the grandchildren turned out! I always say — they're Christians, they're achievers, they're multi- faceted, and they're sweet. Every one of them. Of the 16 who are grown, 15 have graduated or are soon to graduate from college, and a half-dozen of them already have graduate degrees. And in this day and age, there's not a divorce among them. My two children have a long way to go to match their cousins.

My memory of Mother and Daddy that endures is their sitting in the living room in their favorite recliner chairs, reading from their well-worn *Daily Lights,* sipping tea, talking, and praying. As an adult I often would be stretched out on that comfortable sofa Mother had. Daddy would look at Mother with adoration. Mother and Daddy always had somewhat regular family devotions, often concluding with prayer on their knees, but in later years it became something they did morning and night. It was the truest rest I have ever known. As an adult whenever I was home, I would stretch out on the couch and doze while they chatted and prayed. I generally would go to bed first. And later, one of them would come in to rearrange the blanket over me. I felt loved.

We had a big celebration at the farm for their 25th silver wedding anniversary in 1945; Chuck was home from the Navy. We celebrated their 50th golden wedding anniversary a few months early during the summer of 1970, because Lois was able to be there then. Daddy approached both warily but went on as the celebrations progressed to enjoy them thoroughly. One snap in 1970 shows him and grandson Richard sharing a hearty laugh.

In those later years, Mother and Daddy went out to eat often two meals a day. If I were home, Daddy or perhaps Mother would say: "Let's go eat out," as if it were a brand new idea, when, as a matter of fact, they had said the very same thing at the previous meal! And they ranged the countryside: Tom's, at Manly; Rockwell; Nora Springs; and their favorite, Country Kitchen, west of Mason City. If it were a Sunday afternoon, they were sure to go to the cemeteries: Chuck's grave and the Halsor graves at Elmwood in Mason City, for sure, and probably check their own plots and those of the Pipperts in Park Cemetery in Nora Springs. In 1954 they took their first vacation by themselves in years and years — from July 20 to 23, the grand sum of a weekend! In 1959, Mother and Daddy and Uncle Calvin and Aunt Mabel went to the Ozarks by way of Kansas City where they saw Paul and Wava.

One April night in 1974, Daddy called me in Washington and said he and Mother would arrive the next evening at Dulles airport. They came, and for three days I took them everywhere — we ate in the Senate's Family Dining Room at the Capitol, we went to the U.S. Naval Academy at Annapolis, we ate at a German restaurant in Georgetown. And then they flew home.

Easter weekend 1976, their last together, was memorable. Roy and Marie, Gary and his fiancée Karen Werner (four months before their wedding), and I had gone to Mason City. That Saturday, Daddy gave us the grand tour of the neighborhood, and he was at his storytelling finest. He drove past all the farms the folks had lived on, with a story about each. That night, Mother invited Gary and Karen to go into the living room and have their devotions, using her Bible since they hadn't brought one. Then she and Daddy went up to bed, leaving Karen to sleep in the front porch and Gary on the couch. The next morning Daddy was supposed to help cook a breakfast of pancakes at the Hanford church. At dawn I awakened to hear Daddy saying in despair the power had gone off during the night and the alarm hadn't gone off. "Come on," I said. "I'll run you down there. Maybe they're still serving." He protested mildly but we got in the car, and I drove upwards of 100 miles an hour to Hanford. When we got there, everyone else was just gathering, too. For the power had gone off throughout the neighborhood and all were in the same pickle. A little while later the rest of us returned to the church and there was Daddy proudly serving pancakes at the various tables.

Their last years were golden years, and they enjoyed each other's company. After the pain of the early years, this was God's gift to them for perseverance and uprightness.

The Older Three

Chapter 6

THE OLDER THREE

We children were divided into the Older Three — Lois, Chuck and Paul — and the Younger Four — Marie, I, Harriet and Harold. The Folks referred to us that way. There was some rationale on their part: the biggest spread of years between any of us children was the five years between Nos. 3 and 4, Paul and Marie. There was a certain respect, a certain awe, a certain status that we Younger Four attached to the Older Three, and still do.

[I should state at the outset that the events I recall in this chapter are drawn from the memories of a young boy looking on older brothers and a sister who were doing things beyond the comprehension of a boy that age. So, my recollections probably are a dim reflection of what actually happened during that period.]

LOIS, CHUCK, AND PAULY

One of my favorite pictures of our family is one of a youthful Mother and Daddy, a girl with a smile standing behind them, a handsome, dark-haired boy on one of their knees and a mischievous-looking boy on another. Lois, Chuck, and Pauly.

I remember as a boy looking on with adoration when Lois would laughingly remonstrate Chuck or Pauly for saying something risqué. During World War II, when Chuck was home on leave, one of the boys told a story about Jane Russell and twin mountain peaks, and she mildly scolded them. But it was clear she was enjoying it as much as they did — enjoying not necessarily the story but enjoying them.

The Older Three really do have a lock on many of the family secrets. They participated in the California experience the Younger Four didn't. The experiences of the Ladwig place obviously were the starkest to the Older Three. And the experiences of Mother and Daddy with the Grandparents also were most vivid to them.

Lois, the eldest, was born Thursday, December 22, 1921 ("You can remember because it was 12-22-21 — 1-2-2-2-2-1," she said) in a stone house on 'the Pike', now US 18, near Taylor Bridge. Chuck was born in California on March 29, 1924, the only one of us seven children to be born in a hospital, and Pauly 15 months later on Friday, July 3, 1925. Chuck and Pauly were both delivered by Dr. C.C. Violet, who was still making house calls in 1952 at 88. Mother used to say that Chuck's being born on Saturday, as per the old poem, meant that he would have to work hard, and indeed, he did.

After returning to Iowa, the Older Three went to the Portland school, often walking along the Milwaukee tracks between the Ladwig place and school, or on the gravel road and up/down that big hill in front of Grubens. Paul recalls that they would coax Billy Krause to stop and ask Mrs. Gruben for cookies. And they all went on to Mason City High School; Lois in the class of 1938, and Chuck and Paul the class of 1942.

Chuck and Pauly were 15 months apart, the closest of brothers. Paul wasn't Chuck's twin, but his complement. If Chuck kept his clothes tidy outside, Mother says, Pauly was soiled in moments. If Chuck stayed out of trouble, Pauly got into it. They never seemed alike to me, but rather the matched pair. As Paul said of Chuck years later: "Oh yeah. He cleaned a couple of the guys' clock who were picking on me." "I could always talk to him," Paul said of Chuck. "He'd listen to me." I thought, growing up, that they scrapped a lot, and I thought, isn't that too bad. I realized much later how the scrapping merely was the cloak for a tight bond. I learned never to try to intrude my way into that relationship, either. In 1949, after both boys returned home from the military, Paul had a flax field north of the buildings on the home place. Some problem — or so I thought — arose between the two of them over the combining of it, and I made, again, what I thought was a mediating remark to one of them, I can't remember which. But what I do remember is that Chuck told me in a way that I did not misunderstand that it was none of my affair.

Chuck and Pauly were responsible for my becoming a Republican at age 6. It was the 1940 campaign, and Chuck and Pauly had a blue-and-white Wilkie sticker in Lois' Model B Ford. If they were for Wilkie, that was good enough for me. Both boys were skilled with their hands — both took mechanics and woodworking in high school. Both made artful shelves that Mother hung on her walls. Chuck also made a couple of pieces of furniture that Mother kept in the living room — a small upright bookcase, and an interesting magazine rack (shaped with two horizontal shelves and two vertical chambers). It was just my luck as a mechanical illiterate to be sandwiched between brothers Chuck and Paul on the one hand, and Harold, on the other, who were mechanical wizards.

Chuck and Paul both liked to go to the Maple Inn, at the intersection of Maple Drive and SE 4th Street, for ribs. Chuck played the tuba in the Mason City High School band under Carleton Stewart; Pauly, the baritone.

But as the '40s wore on, the Older Three went their separate ways. Lois went off to St. Paul Bible Institute in 1940, Chuck joined the Navy in 1942, and Paul pulled home duty until he went into radio in 1945. They did not spend a lot of time together from then on. But I know now that the separation did not disturb their tightly woven intimacy. I see now, with Chuck and Lois gone too soon, how Paul has been orphaned, and one is no more prepared for that at 65 than at 6.

There is one thing that in an unusual way defines the kind of sons Chuck and Paul were. Both smoked as adults — but never in front of Mother and Daddy (or Big Sister Lois). Daddy once asked Chuck why not. "Because I have too much respect for you," Chuck replied. That is a remarkable tribute. Paul once told me: "I always tried all my life never to do anything in front of the Folks that would hurt or embarrass them."

By contrast: consider the son who brings his girlfriend home on a visit and says, "Mother, we sleep together when we're away so we think it's only honest to do so here," giving great heed to so-called 'honesty' but none to the mother's feelings.

But not always. One day, Chuck, 5, and Pauly, 4, found a can of Prince Albert tobacco in the barn on the Krieger place. "We gotta get to smoking," they said to each other. They soon had fashioned a crude cigarette from a newspaper. Pauly stuck his in his mouth and marched across the road to demand a match from Mother. It didn't work. Later, the boys, again trying to smoke, burned up Daddy's soybean crop for the year that was stacked near the barn. Even Grandpa Pippert and local mogul Hanford MacNider showed up to watch. Paul got sent to bed and recalled later that "Daddy was extremely unhappy."

Lois

I once asked Paul what Lois was like. "She was kind of bossy. Took Chuck and me places and taught us to drive." That really said it — the Big Sister, caring and looking out for her two younger brothers. Lois was brilliant: Mother and Daddy said she always had a book in her hand and generally read one or so in a day. She was loving: as revealed in her traditional closing of her letters, "Lovingly, Lois." As Mother and Marie, whom she called "Sis," frequently pointed out, "Lois was a peacemaker." I know of not one instance in which she had difficulties with anyone. She was highly competent professionally, and missionary executives told me how she was held in high esteem. She arranged overseas tours for the last employer she had, the Christian Medical Society. She was close to Mother and Daddy, and I always thought that next to Mother, there was no one Daddy enjoyed more. More even than Uncle Calvin. In Lois' adult life when her trips home became increasingly fewer, Daddy would keep her up until 1 and 2 in the morning, talking about the old days. Only Lois knew the family lore like Mother and Daddy knew it, and when she died those tales went with her.

As she was growing up, Mother and Daddy permitted something they probably regretted later. They let Lois spend her freshman year in high school with newly married Aunt Ruth and Uncle Arthur in Browerville, Minnesota, far to the north. The rationale for this was unknown — especially since Mother probably could have used help at home and Lois surely must have grown homesick for her little brothers. Paul believes that what may have been an innocuous remark by Uncle Arthur — like, "Why don't you come live with us?" — was taken seriously by Lois and then took on a life of its own. At any rate, Lois and Ruth established a life-long closeness, and both of them, of similar build and temperament, departed this life too early, Ruth at 62 and Lois at 64.

Lois had long braids that she didn't cut until she got to college. She played the violin at Mason City High School and was a member of Carleton L. Stewart's orchestra that won a national championship. Years later, in 1983, we bumped into Stewart at the Holiday Inn one Sunday dinner. She told him what the orchestra had played as its contest piece. After graduating from high school at age 16, she bought a Ford Model B coupe, made in 1931 or 1932, which I always thought looked like a sleek Model A. Lois' Model B had a starter that was hand-pulled from the dash and a choke that was broken off. It was the car that Lois used to teach Chuck and Paul and Jim to drive.

Lois drove it to the Iowa State Brand Creameries on the southwest edge of Mason City where she, Lois Gephardt, Marcella Wang, and Francis Emmert wrapped quarters and pounds of butter by hand. It was an immaculate sight — rows of young women dressed in white, taking a pound or a quarter of butter off a conveyor belt and wrapping it crisply, quickly. Occasionally, Lois stopped off on her way home to see Grandpa and Grandma Pippert, whom Lois resembled in build. When Grandma died in 1961, she left Lois her clothes that she could use.

At that time, Cerro Gordo County's sheriff was Tim Phalen, a big, affable guy, popular. Marie and I used to sing:

> There was a tavern in the town, in the town,·
> Until Tim Phalen closed it down, closed it down.

Daddy said that when Tim Phalen would see Lois' Model B parked uptown, he would wait until she came back, one time even sitting in it. Another fellow who had his eye on Lois was James R. Brown, later the County Attorney.

But her heart was set on St. Paul Bible Institute, for she had determined in her heart at age 12 that she wanted to be a missionary to Africa, as Mother had felt called to be. So, after working two years at the creamery, Lois went off to SPBI. She quickly was elected class officer, got a job at Montgomery Ward on University Boulevard, and met Jim. Jim, was a member of the Alliance who had felt the call to South America as a youngster of 12. Soon Lois wrote home that she had joined the South America Prayer Band. So they courted where SPBI students in those days courted — by going to the South America Prayer band on Friday nights. I assume they went to Como Park to neck.

In those days, SPBI occupied a grand old three-story red-brick mansion-type building at 1361 Englewood Avenue. The male students lived on third floor, the young women on second floor, and the classrooms and other offices were on first floor, along with the switchboard (telephone NEstor 7861). They all ate family-style in a large room that once had been a tiny gym. While Lois and Jim were students, Lowell Young graduated and took a pastorate, and Aunt-to-be Dorothy went for a year as well. SPBI had a fine male quartet made up of Ray Ashmun, Dave Husted, and two Mason City boys, Ralph Williams, and Joe Dahl.

But the man of her hour was Jim. He was from Oklahoma City, the oldest of four children to W.S. and Lillie Comstock, who lived at 1411 NW 14th. Then came Walter Starr Jr., better known as Mickey, an Eagle Scout who got into World War II by lying about his age, and became a career military man; Pearl Marie, who we suspected had a crush on Pauly; and Roy, of whom you'll hear much more later. Jim and Lois obviously were in love, and Jim came to spend the summer on the farm. One vivid scene sticks in my mind. Jim was taking a shower in the milk house when he called me to come see his appendectomy scar. My reaction was a. startle — not so much the scar, but at the tender age of seven or eight I had never seen pubic hair! Paul called him "Don Jaime," Spanish for Sir James. They rollicked a lot. One day they were cleaning out the east cowbarn, pulling the manure spreader behind the John Deere A. In their glee, they clipped off the post of the main gate, leaving it to dangle for years.

In a way, Jim had it rough. What brothers feel that their sister's boyfriend deserves her?

Uncle Carl was a big Minnesota Gopher fan in those days, and Mother rode along with him to the Twin Cities on game days a time or two to see Lois, Carl carefully never exceeding the wartime speed limit of 35. Only rarely did we drive to St. Paul to see Lois. Now it takes a little more than two hours, but it took Daddy five hours going up old US 65, getting lost in South St. Paul, inching up Snelling to University and finally to SPBI. Daddy was never fond of making family trips. When Lois graduated in 1943, Mother suggested that Grandma Pippert go along to the ceremony with us. Daddy had a 'conniption': but at the end of the day — for we made the round trip to St. Paul in a single day — Daddy told Mother how much he had enjoyed it.

Daddy wanted Lois to wait a while after graduation to get married, and she did, but only until autumn. Jim arrived by train in Nora Springs from his pastorate in Arlington, Texas, and on October 24, 1943, Jim and Lois were married. A reluctant Daddy walked with Lois down the aisle. Lowell Young, now the Mason City pastor, performed the ceremony, Paul and Marie were the attendants, and Dorothy sang. Chuck was in the Navy, unable to attend. The next summer, Lois came home, and on July 22, 1944, their eldest, Barton Lowell, was born at Park Hospital in Mason City. I liked the name — I had been reading a book with the name 'Barton' in it, and Lowell, of course, was for Lowell Young. Jim gave him his initial nickname, 'Barry', which in adult years gave way to 'Bart'.

During the early years of their marriage, Jim and Lois spent a lot of time in Mason City. When Mother had her heart attacks, in late 1946 and 1947, Jim and Lois and their growing family moved to Mason City for a while and lived in a house in northwest Mason City. Lois even worked a stretch at Decker's. One autumn Lois was home, and she wanted to take lunch down to Daddy and Chuck on the 110. Since no car was available, Lois bridled Silver and crawled on. Silver was not broken very well, and refusing to be reined in, she carried through several fields a pregnant and utterly exasperated Lois.

The summer of 1950 was a traumatic one for all of us. By this time Lois and Jim had served their first term as missionaries in Colombia. Marie and Roy were getting married in August, and Jim and Roy went to Texas to buy Roy a Chevrolet from Jim's friends Ed and Hazel Williams, who were Chevy dealers. On the way back, they had a car accident in Kansas and Jim broke his leg [It was a very bad day: Daddy had gone to a funeral, Mrs. Clausen's? Donnie Gruben was killed in a car accident near Portland. The word came about Jim and Roy. That night, the Herts came to visit and our black chow, Mickey, tore into their youngest daughter Marjorie. It could have been terrible]. The ambulance which picked up Jim and Roy was driven by Earl Torneden, our distant cousin from Grandpa Pippert's side. So Jim performed the ceremony with his leg in a cast. That fall, Jim, taking young son Jay with him and his leg still in a cast, went to Taylor University in Upland, Indiana. Lois stayed at the farm. Barry started school that fall at Portland No. 2, the third generation of our family to attend there. The spring semester, both Comstock couples attended Taylor and lived in the Marion area.

But most important, three times Lois and Jim and family went to South America as missionaries — to Colombia under sponsorship of the Latin America Mission 1947-1950, and under sponsorship of the Oriental Missionary Society, to Brazil 1954-1959 and Colombia in the 1960s. The separation was long. During my three years in Israel, I came back to the States several times. Lois would be gone for three to five years and would not get home or call home even once. But Mother didn't mind, for she saw her lifelong dream come true in her eldest. Lois was her surrogate.

Between terms, Lois, now the mother of six, took classes at Friends University in Wichita, Kansas, and graduated in 1965, as usual, near the top of her class with a triple major in languages and a member of the elite Order of the Tower.

She never stopped learning. She took nurses training. Back in the Dallas suburb of Carrollton in the 1980s, she went to work for the Christian Medical Society. From time to time, I met people who knew Lois in one capacity or another, and always, unfailingly, they spoke of her competence, her good cheer, her kindness.

My last week in Israel was in June 1986, the very time that Lois suffered an aneurysm. Elizabeth and I flew to Dallas at the end of July to see Lois, and I took along some of my myriad family scrapbooks to show her. It appeared then that she would recover but it would take time. Still she showed glints of recognition and delight at the old pictures. She had told Marie she wanted to sit down and have a long chat with me. It didn't happen, but I am consoled that Elizabeth did get to meet her. On December 13, 1986, a Saturday night, the call came from Paul. She was gone.

So our shrinking family gathered in Carrollton on Tuesday. Our final hymn, amid the tears, was:

> Joy to the world!
> The Lord is come;
> Let earth receive her King;
> Let ev'ry heart prepare Him room,
> And Heav'n and nature sing,
> And Heav'n and nature sing,
> And Heav'n and nature sing.

CHUCK

Chuck was the eldest son, the big brother, the acknowledged leader of us children, the prince of the family. His loss was far, far too soon, and it is a loss, three decades later, from which we never have recovered. I know the loss I feel; I can't even fathom the loss that Paul, who was like a twin to him, must live with.

He was handsome, he was dapper, he was a war hero, he was volatile, he was generous to a fault, and he mentored us. He loved to talk, always with great animation — arched eyebrows and elaborate gesture. He loved to argue, although Mother, always drawing the best conclusion about her children, said he often took the other side just for the sake of the argument. One night, I believe the day Frank Emmert got married, Chuck was asserting that it was impossible to love the child of a miscarriage inasmuch as the parent had never seen the child — for in order to love something, in his view, you had to have actually sensed it. One night Chuck and Jim talked and talked with heat over when the soul enters the body — a precursor of the 1981 Senate hearing on the bill that would declare that life began at conception. One Sunday noon, one of the last times we all were together, he made a sweeping gesture with his hand in the living room as he was making a point, just as Marie came in carrying a plate of food. Chuck caught the plate with his hand swinging upward and sent food aflying. He was embarrassed.

He was sensitive. During the summer of 1951 he had a young, hired man named Stan Fleming, of Iowa Falls. Stan and I did a lot of things together; that fall I went off to Iowa University, and Stan, Ellsworth J.C. in his hometown of Iowa Falls. A year later, at Thanksgiving time, Chuck approached me at home one evening and told me Stan had committed suicide. Stan had written me that he had been in a car accident in which his girlfriend suffered a broken neck and serious internal problems. Then Chuck said: "Don't tell the Folks." They had really liked Stan, and Chuck didn't want them to feel badly. Another time, I was 18, home from college for Christmas and had had a date the night before. He and I were cleaning out the chicken house — or something — on his farm east of Rock Falls. I made a mildly lascivious remark, thinking he would laugh. He scolded me and gave me a lecture on how to treat women.

He also was proud, proud that he was a good farmer, proud of some of the things he could do — like, Stan Fleming told me, back up a 4-wheel wagon behind a tractor (the trick: go back and forth in small bites, like a skier in reverse).

One day Chuck and I were out combining, he on one combine and I on another. I was probably 15 or 16, he was ten years older. My machine broke down, and being mechanically inept while he was a whiz, I walked across the field to fetch him. I told him I was broke down. "Fix it," he said, and kept going. He had a new Oliver 70 tractor with a four-row cultivator, and one summer I estimated I cultivated a row from Mason City to Chicago with it. Chuck made me keep a long pole on the tractor, and if I so much as covered up a leaf of a stalk of corn, I had to stop and use the pole — so I wouldn't waste time by getting off the tractor — to knock the dirt off. He taught me how to plow or plant or cultivate a straight row: focus on something at the end of the field and not keep fine tuning one's direction as one went along. He showed me how to get a wide piece of machinery through a narrow gate — like getting the 4-row cultivator mounted on his Oliver 70 through the gate by the corn crib on the home place. (Back the tractor alongside the fence so that the rear wheel is next to the post holding the gate and the left side of the cultivator is already through the gate, then brake the left tire and spin the tractor on around and through the gate. The rest of the cultivator will easily clear the other side of the gate.)

I loved being around him. I copied him. In his high school graduation picture, he was wearing a smart-looking green hopsack suit and a brown polka dot tie, with his mouth in a small 'Mona Lisa' smile. The next time the photographer came to country school to take pictures, I very consciously wore the same kind of a smile with my hair combed the same way as his. I used his expressions — "table-top level," for one. "It's New York, N.Y.," he told me, "not New York City." To this day I write the date, as did he, as 29 March 1924. When I would help him in the field while he was living a mile north of the home place, when Saturday night came, he would sometimes take me out to see the Mason City Legionnaires play baseball, with Red Rose or Mully Fredericks (of Nora Springs) pitching. For instance, here is one typical entry in my diary for Saturday, March 26, 1949, when I was 14: "About 11, Chuck came. I went up to Chuck's. After dinner I came and got silage for him and then helped him do his chores. At 8, he brought me home, went to Norie and then Chuck and Billie came back for a visit."

If it sounds like Chuck was central in our family life, he was. If it sounds like he got a lot of work out of me, he did, and that included sweeping out his white Ford V-8 or the Dodge pick-up every time he had a date. But I didn't care. When I won the American Legion Medal for social science at the high school graduation at Roosevelt Fieldhouse, he stood and cheered. If I gave a talk at church, he came to hear me. He seemed to me to know about everything — from him I first learned that Castro was overrunning Batista in Cuba in 1958, and he knew the significance. I remember his saying how much he liked W. Somerset Maugham's *The Razor's Edge*. He liked Jack Paar's Tonight show. One September, I was thrilled when he drove me to Iowa City to start my sophomore year at the university. And my final May at Iowa, in 1954, he came down to pick me up. Even as late as 1954, when I was 20 and a senior in college, my diary records, "Chuck, I played croquet," or "Chuck, I played catch." The very last time I saw him was at Mother and Daddy's 40th anniversary in November 1960, and I flew home from Pierre to attend. Marie took me aside during the afternoon and told me to ask Mother and Daddy to take me to the airport for my return flight, because she knew I would surely ask Chuck to take me. He met, my wife aside, two of the loves of my life, the only ones in my family to do so.

He always was there at the time of need. One summer Hugh Hughes was having trouble getting his hay in. So Chuck took Daddy and me and went over and made short work of it for Hughie. One summer afternoon in 1947, Chuck and Daddy were cutting oats with a binder when the word came that Billy's sister-in-law, Amy Haight, who was married to Paul Poppen, had died suddenly. "We were just together last night," Chuck said in shock. And off he went. Later, he took Daddy's power binder over the gravel roads to Poppens to help cut oats. When our cousin Jovetta died at 25 — nine years to the day before Chuck —

he sat up with her for several of her last nights. When someone needed blood, Chuck gave it — and then came home and would shovel a load of corn or whatever without taking a break. When Mother was having one of her heart attacks and the children gathered, what she wanted to hear was her sons pray for her — and she got her desire.

Mother said that Charles — to her, he was always Charles as a little boy, always asked her to sing a song while she was rocking him. "Sing it again, Mother," he'd say.

> When I fear my faith would fail, Christ will hold me fast:
> When the tempter would prevail, He can hold me fast...
> I am precious in his sight, He will hold me fast;
> Those He saves are His delight, He will hold me fast...
> He will hold me fast, He will hold me fast;
> For my saviour loves me so, He will hold me fast.

Those songs were not forgotten, for when he grew up Chuck was Mother's great protector, and he confronted anyone — anyone — he felt had been unkind to her.

Chuck showed his bent for mechanics early. We had an old truck, a Chevy, I believe, that had been setting in the grove for some time. Chuck and a buddy got it going and set off for Mason City so they could work on it in Mechanics class in high school. I remember yet that Daddy looked out the front-room window, saw the truck going down with Chuck in the driver's seat, laughing with a sense of accomplishment, and then Daddy broke into a laugh himself as he pointed out Chuck's delight to Mother. That truck's box, by the way, sat for years afterward in the barn in front of the stanchions on the west side.

It was the dark days of World War II. Chuck attended Mason City Junior College in the fall of 1942, but only for a few weeks. He joined the Navy and marched down Federal Avenue in a patriotic, but sad, Navy Day parade on October 27. Before he left, the Alliance young people had a going-away party for him at the farm. It was here that Chuck "took his stand for the Lord," something Mother clung to for the rest of her days.

He took his boot training at Great Lakes, and then went to trade school at Butler University in Indianapolis, Indiana, to study to be a signalman. I remember yet Mother saying that the average life of a signalman on a ship in battle was 18 or 19 seconds (Chuck also pointed out to me that in the Navy, it's ships' not 'boats', and servicemen go 'overseas' while civilians go 'abroad').

After this was over, he unexpectedly was assigned to Lighter-than-Air (blimps), trained in Glynco, Georgia, and won his wings. Years and years later, I saw one of those huge blimp hangars at Glynco while covering Jimmy Carter vacationing off Brunswick, and Marie's Gordie's office at MAP International was in one of the remaining hangars.

After each round of training, Chuck would come home on leave. He was smartly attired in his dress blues or dress whites. He was proud, and so were we. Generally he had ten-day leaves, spending five days traveling (by train, of course), and five days at home. One morning, Daddy came to the house and said someone was walking up the half-mile gravel road from US 18. I don't know how that caught Daddy's eye, but it turned out to be Chuck. During one leave, he attended the Gleaners class meeting at the PG&E, but left early to catch his train. "Bless him, Lord, and make him a blessing," they sang as he walked erectly out, and Mother cried.

When he finished Glynco, he knew that he was going to be stationed in South America, but where he was uncertain. So he left us a list of ten cities, and told us that he would make some kind of an allusion in his letters, which were censored. He wrote he needed some "size·7" socks; and we checked the list to see city No. 7 — Fortaleza, Brazil, which, indeed, turned out to be where he had been assigned. Another time Aunt Esther heard first from him, with a new address. I remember yet Mother trying to take it down over the phone from Auntie Esther. Part of the address was '90' something or other. Esther said, "He has drawn a line through the zero, from the upper right-hand corner to the lower left-hand corner." Actually, I suppose he simply dashed off a line through his zero as many people do, but Esther and Mother, given the secrecy of World War II, thought Chuck was using a special code.

During his twelve months in South America, he wrote home often. He made photo albums. He sent gifts — the wings he had won, two alligator-leather purses for mother, a lace tablecloth from Brazil decorated with cherubs (which Marie has and uses only for special occasions), a book, *Puss in Boots,* for Harriet. One of Mother's favorite photos, now hanging in my home, is a black-and-white snapshot that Chuck took of a vulture in a dead tree. He explained that when the vulture starts perching in a tree, the tree soon dies. His letters arrived faithfully, interesting, always on U.S. Navy letterheads, and they now are in notebooks in the hands of his two sons. One time when Chuck was home on leave, Marie had the mumps, and when Chuck got back to South America, he got the mumps! As a crew member of a blimp, Chuck would go aloft for up to 24 hours and peer for

German subs along the South American and African coasts. He got two battle stars for his wings, but he never told us how he got them.

When World War II was about over, Chuck finished his tour in South America and came home in the dead of winter. He was reassigned back to being a signalman and had to go to boot training all over again at Newport, Rhode Island. When Uncle Jess and Dorothy got married in June 1944, she had to keep working in the Twin cities for three months while he was on duty in New York. That fall, Chuck, who had been home on leave, and Dorothy rode the train cross-country back east where Chuck reported for duty and Dorothy was reunited with Jess. As the war ended, he was assigned to the maiden crew of an aircraft carrier, the USS Lake Champlain. It quickly was converted to a troop carrier, and Chuck made several trips across the Atlantic bringing American boys home from Europe. One trip, the Lake Champlain had a mechanical problem about the time of a forecast of a heavy storm. So, in order to get back to port quickly, the captain poured on the steam, and the Lake Champlain set a speed record for crossing the Atlantic, a record which held until the Queen Elizabeth set a new one some time later. The Lake Champlain later was used to pick up from the Atlantic some of the early astronauts. Years later, before it was scrapped, I went to the Philadelphia Navy Yards to climb all over the Lake Champlain.

Finally, Chuck was discharged in January 1946, and he came home and indicated he wanted to farm. The first year, he rented 160 acres a mile north of Kensett on US 65. That involved hauling machinery 30 miles round-trip. Once he drove the McCormick-Deering 22-36, now on rubber wheels, home from Kensett. It took him five hours. The second year, 1947, he rented Uncle Calvin's place — who had just retired — the Davidson place at Portland and George Senior's 40 on the Rock Falls road. I don't have good memories of that year. It was a rough year weather-wise, and it was tough getting the field work done. It seemed that Uncle Earl and Uncle Calvin were on Chuck's case with some frequency. But it also was about the time that Pat, Uncle Earl's youngest and the apple of his eye, said Chuck took her dancing at the Surf.

Meanwhile, he was beginning to date Wilma Poppen, who lived on a farm southeast of Mason City and also had graduated in 1942, No. 3 in her class. Chuck called her Billy, then 'Bill'. Daddy always remarked about her 'snappy' dark eyes. When they went out, Chuck would get all dressed up, his belt buckle rakishly off to one side, a light tan fedora cocked at an angle, a white scarf. And he assigned me to clean out the car every time. Now and then they would go to the Alliance church on a Sunday night. And in February 1948, they got married in a ceremony at the Poppen home. As they had done for Lois, Paul and Marie were the attendants. The first few years Chuck and Billy lived a mile north of us, so they frequently came down to see Mother and Daddy in the evenings and we worked together in the fields. This was one of the times that Chuck told me to "fix it." Another time, in the summer of 1952, Chuck and Billy helped me stuff envelopes for a mailing to all incoming University of Iowa freshmen about the Inter-Varsity chapter. By 1953, Chuck and Billy and Richard and Greg had moved east of Rock Falls, where Paul and Helen Douglas (see Alliance Gospel Tabernacle) were next-door neighbors and daughter Margaret babysat for them. By 1955, Chuck had bought 160 acres near Stewartville, Minnesota. I remember it vividly because I came home from Minneapolis where I was working with UP to see Joani Ridgeway, my love when I graduated from Iowa who was from New Hampton. Daddy and Chuck had just come back from Stewartville on that Saturday night when I hustled down to New Hampton to see her.

During these years I was working with UP in South Dakota. He wrote me once a year or so. As I look at the letters now, they are breezy, informative, not profound. And dull they ain't! The year before he died, Chuck came out to check on cattle, and I remember he sat in the Hamilton living room and talked to Jane E. and her folks about the merits of range-fed and corn-fed cattle. I thought he seemed agitated.

The call came to the UP bureau in the State Capitol on January 26, 1961, about 10 to 9. It was Uncle Calvin. "Chuck was in a fatal accident last night," he said. I asked him who, thinking he meant one of the little boys for subconsciously I thought Chuck could do anything and was invulnerable to such things as accidents. "It was Chuck," he said... I wandered down to the Capitol coffee shop in a daze, and called Keith Johnson, a parishioner at my church in Harrold and a road contractor, to see if he would fly me home, which he did later that morning. I went back up to the bureau and ripped the wire. There, on the wire even before Uncle Calvin called, was a story that moved about 6:45 a.m. about the latest Minnesota traffic fatalities, including Chuck. I had missed it. About 9:30 a.m., Billy called in a soft, drained voice to tell me Chuck had been killed, apparently thinking that I did not know. When we all gathered at home before the funeral, Mother asked Lois to read from *Daily Light,* which she and Daddy always used. The entry for that day started:

> For I have no pleasure in the death of him that dieth.
> (Eze. 18:32)

As we all drove to Stewartville that bitterly cold winter day and turned the corner to drive into the farm, Daddy noted that Chuck had all his fall plowing done and his new 64-foot pole corn crib was full.

Mother's Christmas letter that year summed up his life: "He left us with so very, very much — a legacy of fearless courage and unexcelled strength, hard work and high hopes, a continual striving for perfection, a fine family, and that which we who loved him know about best, a tender and loving heart."

An amazing thing had occurred as I drove to Pierre Riggs High School that morning to tell Jane E. that Chuck had died. The car radio was on, and the song that was playing was the "Sevenfold Amen" benediction:

A-men! A-men! A-men! A-men! A-men! A-men! A-men!

Paul

One time Mother had led family devotions — and this would have been relatively recently and concluded with all of us joining in the Lord's Prayer. As I sat there, I knew what was coming. And sure enough, it did. Now we all knew that we used the version that said: "Forgive us our trespasses as we forgive those who trespass against us," rather than "Forgive us our debts, as we forgive our debtors." So, we're rolling along in unison and get to that section. Mother, eyes tightly sealed, says earnestly, "Forgive us our trespasses—" and Paul, of course, says, "Forgive us our debts—" then pauses a split second, and with the most explicit timing, as if he equally earnestly wants to correct his mistake, proceeds to say, not "as we forgive our debtors," but "as we forgive our trespassers—" Of course, "trespassers" appears in neither version. Well, we finally finish, and I look up, and Mother's shoulders are convulsed in hushed laughter. Mother didn't laugh a lot, but when she did, it was generally Paul who made her do it.

I can't begin to count the times I have seen Paul twit Mother about something and Mother in turn admonish Paul by shaking her finger at him. It wasn't until years later that I began to suspect that what was going on here was a gargantuan game the two of them were playing, mostly with the rest of us as the unwitting bystanders.

If there was a vote taken throughout the family as to who had brought the most delight, the most popular scion of the clan, it surely would be Paul, hands down. He had a mischievous look as a little boy, and he hasn't lost it as a grandpa. It's who he is. He is verbal, always playing with malapropisms, and mispronunciations. "Poor old Grandpaw," he calls himself to his grandsons. The fun-loving only partly masks as hard a work ethic as any of us in the family has, an utter scrupulousness and commitment to honesty and punctuality. He gave the best advice I have ever heard a parent give. Sitting on our sofa in Jerusalem in 1985, overlooking Mount Zion, he said: "you can't discipline more than you have (love) in the bank."

The stories about Paul are legion, if not legend. Even Mother, proud of her even-handedness ("I love all my children the same…") admitted he got more spankings than any of the other children. Our family has always been accident-prone, and my favorite story involved Paul as a boy. Pauly was playing outside when he ran into a fence. A piece of rusty woven wire ran into his eye, and actually pried the eyeball loose from its socket and pulled it out of his head. Our hired man, old Andrew Zing, worked it out. Pauly ran into the house, his eyeball dangling. Indulging myself a bit of hyperbole, and literary license, I theorized that Pauly must have held the eyeball in his fingers and pointed it toward the house in order to see how to get there. Eventually Paul was taken to Nora Springs and then to Dr. Chenoweth in Mason City, who administered ether to him.

He wasn't above any kind of prank. There had been a spate of suicides in the neighborhood, often by hanging, and one time Paul told Marie and me that that night when we crawled up in the haymow in the darkness to throw down hay, we would bump into the body swinging on a hay rope.

As a boy Pauly won the Portland Township spelling contest, and Mrs. Davidson summoned him to the Portland story for daily rehearsal sessions in preparation for the county spelling bee. She enticed him by 'examining' the contents of 1-cent Guess What bars. Paul soon learned he couldn't lose. En route to the county contest, Daddy promised a trip to Des Moines if Paul came out on top. He didn't.

Pauly also took a high school course in cooking. It was not as foolish as it may have sounded, particularly in these days of feminism which have done more to liberate men from traditional tasks than to liberate women. And Paul also is a superb gourmet cook now. Paul played the piano, with even more gusto as an adult. I'll never forget him sitting at the upright playing "San Antonio Rose." He was a crack checkers player, often challenging the old men in Central Park or at the Y. He claimed to be undefeated in Monopoly, and I'm sure he was. Once at home we and the Carrs were playing a new game called 'Pit', named for the grain market in which the point is to establish a 'corner' on a grain. "Corner on corn!" Marvin shouted in winning the first hand. The next hand Paul won. "Wheater on wheat!" he shouted.

After they graduated from high school in 1942, Chuck went into the Navy, and it fell to Paul to stay home and farm. So, while most of the other fellows were off to war, Paul was home on the basis of 3-A deferments. Viewed from this vantage point, it must have been tough on him. Viewed from the vantage point of the folks, it provided Dad with help and also protected their other elder son from the steadily mounting casualties. One cousin-in-law, Irene's husband Robert Widdrington, was killed in action. So it was not an easy time. When Paul finally left home in the late summer of 1945, shades of Grandpa Pippert, he collected $25 from the folks as a farewell for his three years of helping them farm.

So, Paul stayed home, and, among other things, introduced what he called "high-speed cultivating" to Cerro Gordo County.

Daddy had a new John Deere Model A, complete with power lift. So Paul would put the A in 4th gear, or 5th, go streaking down the rows of corn or beans, come to the end of the field, and then, simultaneously, all in one elongated motion: kick the power lift with his foot, with the help of a knob on the steering wheel spin the John Deere around, skip two rows, hit the next two roads with deadly precision, kick the power lift to drop the cultivator, and go speeding down the field again, never missing a lick. (The evidence is unclear how much he plowed out.) I remember Daddy standing in the yard and laughing with Mother at how Paul was totally intimidating Clarence Steil who was out arduously cultivating with a team of horses, stopping at the end of each row to lift manually first one section of the cultivator out of the ground and then the other, turning around, and then reversing the process.

One day in about 1944 Paul broke his arm cranking the 22-36 (as I also was to do six years later). The Folks were up town. With his arm still in a cast, Paul with one-arm somehow turned the flywheel to start the brand-new John Deere Model A and took it out in the newly clipped hemp field for a spin. The rear wheels were still set in close, and by dang, Paul tipped the tractor over. He crawled off, went over, cranked the 22-36, which hadn't been touched since he broke his arm, and pulled the John Deere upright.

But Paul did more than just farm. He, Russ Bauer, and George Emmert rode bicycles up town to Pattee's, the ice cream shop near the viaduct on East State Street. I went along one time and ate two heaping pints of ice cream — more than a quart in all. But it also was pretty clear he was doing more than just going to Pattee's. He sang in the mixed quartet with Marvin Carr, Elaine Adelsman, and Maybelle Adelsman — until, he said years later, Rev. Young kicked him off for smoking.

One day Paul and one of the Comstock boys — Jim or Roy — were working on Lois' Model B Ford, which frequently had a plugged fuel line. The solution to this problem was to disconnect the fuel line at the carburetor, take off the gasoline cap, and blow into the tank. On this day, Paul had the hood lifted and was looking at the carburetor and shouting to either Jim or Roy in back of the car, "Blow! Blow!" And then, "Keep blowing! Blow!" The only problem was that Paul hadn't disconnected the fuel line and was having a jolly time watching Jim or Roy futilely blow themselves red in the face. It was during this era that Paul went to Medicine Lake and didn't come home when he was supposed to, leading to a dramatic religious crisis for me. Monday night came, and Paul called from the bus depot. When Lois and I picked him up, Lois, the Big Sister, saw it first — the bandage on his forehead, covering the stitches from the injuries when Don Williams' car hit a streetcar in the Twin Cities, presumably when they should have been at the youth service! I remember that one Saturday night, he and George Emmert drove to Austin for a Mohawk game. Sunday morning came, and Paul wasn't home yet. About that time, Uncle Al called to say that Dick and Paul were together there. George had come home without them.

One of Paul's friends from this period was Sig Heinz, son of Rev. F.A. Heinz, a Lutheran pastor. That friendship started a process that shaped Paul's life. Sig had a brother, Al (for Albin), who was an announcer at KGLO. Paul became friends with Al, too, and Al came out for Sunday dinner (I remember that Daddy, in talking to Al, speculated that some day, scientists would be able to retrieve radio signals from time past. So people could tune in on, say, Orson Welles' dramatic end-of-the-world broadcast from the 1930s. An incredible thought! But I have heard this same thing speculated on only recently, so Daddy, once again, was not so far off). Paul was drawn to radio.

During the war years, Paul had gone to Echo, Minnesota, where Uncle Les was pastor, to thresh oats and make some money harvesting. In early September 1945, Paul went to Clark, South Dakota, to help in the potato harvest. The trip shaped his life.

Paul took the bus to Minneapolis and the train to Clark. standing outside the hotel, he met a fellow who told him about the potato harvest where he could make 70 cents an hour, working perhaps 14-hour days. Paul began filling sacks with spuds, was quickly promoted to loading sacks on a flatbed truck, and then to truck driver. One rainy day, he and his friend went to Watertown, a few miles east, to cruise and go to Kreiser's drug store. Visiting KWAT, Paul was invited to read some copy and was offered a job. He turned it down once, but back in Watertown on the next rainy day, he was offered it again. He accepted at $79 a month, starting in October. So, the rest of the year, Paul announced on KWAT. That October 1945 was the beginning of a nearly 45-year career.

When January 1946 came (the same month University of Chicago genius William Heirens, 17, kidnapped and killed Susanne Degnan}, Paul was drafted. After basic training at Camp Robinson, Arkansas, and Fort Lawton, Washington, awaiting shipment overseas, he was assigned to Camp Carson, Colorado, and soon became the staff announcer for the camp's broadcast on KVOR. In 1947, after Paul was discharged, he enrolled at Mason City Junior College as I was starting the ninth grade at Roosevelt Junior High School. Paul would take me to Roosevelt on his way to JC. Recall, please, Paul's oft-proclaimed commitment to punctuality. Morning after morning, however, we would go speeding in Paul's Model A into town, past the Maple Inn onto then-gravel SE 4th Street, turn south, bounce into the air as we crossed the Milwaukee tracks, turn right on SE 12th street to Roosevelt — and late. I was late so many times, I had to stay after school. It got to be such a habit that I stopped making an excuse to Genevieve, the secretary, even on a particular morning when there might have been extenuating circumstances, and she routinely would reach for her red pad. Paul went out for football as a lineman, and played one full quarter, even though later he said he took a hard hit and couldn't remember doing so.

In January, 1948, station KSMN (Komplete Sports, Music, News} went on the air, at a station built on the site of where Daddy went to Portland 3 country school, and Paul was on the maiden staff. Paul's career was under way for good. One day Paul was driving to work in the Dodge pick-up and Marie was going along to bring it back. At the corner, Paul braked, and the brake started to drag. The pickup eased into the ditch — and tipped over. On May 13, 1948, I went with Paul to the station and watched the first news of the proclamation of the rebirth of Israel coming over the UP wire. KSMN soon moved the studio to the Weir building, designed by Frank Lloyd Wright, on the southwest corner of State and Federal. Paul moved steadily upward — in 1950 to KMA, Shenandoah, where he was a newscaster. I was attending the University of Iowa then, and I would proudly check the radio listings in the Des Moines Register for KMA to find "10 p.m. — News, P. Pippert." While there, he took classes at Tarkio College in Missouri and Paulette Kay was born. And in 1954, on to KCMO,

Kansas City, where he eventually became a farm broadcaster. By the time he was done, he would have become one of the nation's senior, most decorated farm broadcasters.

We need to backtrack just a bit. While Paul was working at KSMN, he began dating Wava Withers, a student at LaJames College of Beauty Culture. (Years later, when I dated Linda Eddy of Swaledale, I told Daddy, "Daddy, all four of us boys have dated girls from south of town: Chuck and Billy, from southeast of Mason City; Paul and Wava, from Chapin; Harold and Sandy, from Rockwell, and me!" "Remarkable," he said.) Paul dated Wava in the legendary Dodge pickup for a while, but by the time they married in January 1951, he was driving a Hudson with a push-button starter. I remember because it wouldn't start that morning.

If Paul's travel was restricted during the war, he made up for it later. As a farm broadcaster, he went abroad nine times, to the Soviet Union three times, to the 1972 Munich Olympics (and was there 30 minutes before the terrorists killed the Israelis), to Eastern Europe in 1976, to China in 1979, to Scandinavia and Hungary in 1983, to Israel in 1984 and 1986, and very frequently to Washington. With the family they took frequent trips West, to New England, and sundry other places. Wava, meanwhile, operated her own shop, Lovely Lady Salon, for nearly 25 years. And on the eve of his retirement, Wava became the first woman to win the Meritorious Service Award from the National Association of Farm Broadcasters.

Paul collected a case full of trophies. He became a 32nd degree Mason and a Shriner. He was 1962 president of the Kansas City Livestock Market Boosters Club. In 1963 he edited *Chats*, the NAFB publication. He won the National Future Farmers Association's Distinguished Service Award in 1967. He won a trip to Switzerland as the 'outstanding farm broadcaster of the year' in a contest sponsored by Ciba-Geigy chemicals. When he fulfilled a life-long ambition by graduating from the Reisch School of Auctioneering in 1967, he quipped, typically: "It was an essentiality of the highest mandantorianism." The biggest tribute of all, however, was Paulette, who followed her father into broadcasting.

The Next Generation

Lois

Lois had six children. Their cousins achieved like Lois' children did, but Lois' did it first — getting college educations, and showing the versatility of their genes, winding up in a wide swathe of the professions. Most of them followed their father (and uncles) to Taylor.

The eldest grandchild, Barton Lowell (Saturday, 7/22/1944-?), appropriately, was born in Mason City. He married Marilyn Louise Stucky (6/11/1944-) on 6/11/1967, and two months later she got her RN from Indianapolis General Hospital. He started school at Portland 2 and concluded at Kansas University medical school and is now a pediatrician in Berrien Springs, Michigan. They have two children, Monique Janee (4/20/1969-), a fourth-generation student (starting with Uncle Les) at Taylor, and Jared Trent (12/1/1972-). Mother had a favorite story about Bart. She had stitched a sewing machine needle deep into her finger, and she always told how carefully Bart removed the needle.

Jay Alan (Sunday, 4/14/1946-) married Taylor co-ed Shirley Ann Lee (1/19/1947-) on 6/20/1970. He graduated from Asbury Seminary, pastored, serving at one time as the education minister for the United Methodist Church in Carrollton, Texas, a Dallas suburb, with the largest Methodist adult Sunday School program in the country. They have four children: Kimberly Faye (3/29/1971-), who won a full scholarship at the University of New Orleans; Angela Denise (5/17/1974-); Bradley Alan (11/15/1975-); and Leann Michele (5/26/1978-). Jay, multi-talented, was so gifted a photographer that he could have become a professional, instead he chose the ministry — and in mid-career became a certified public accountant. Shirley became a real estate salesman.

Laurence Gard Comstock (Tuesday, 9/30/1947-), Lois' No. 3 son, returned to finish college at North Texas State at age 40 as an honor student in political science. He married Francis 'Faye' Harrison on 8/11/1973, and they have three children, Joshua Benjamin 8/?/1976-), Adam David (6/21/1978-), and Rebecca.

Dale Brent (Tuesday, 2/22/1949-), the final son and computer whiz, graduated from Azusa and married Margaret Ann 'Peggy' Bailey (2/14/1947-) on 2/5/1971. They have two sons, Brent Jonathan (12/13/1973-) and Bart James 2/8/1979-) More about these two boys when we talk about Chuck's grandchildren. No one ever accused Dale of being rigid. He switched companies as fast as the seasons change, always moving up. And he went on for his master's.

Lois had four sons and then two daughters. Brooke Renee (Monday, 12/21/1953-), who married a career soldier, Edwin Evert Bruner (8/12/1943-) on 6/6/1975, and lived in Germany during most of the 1980s. They had five children, though losing one: Chad Evert (8/28/1976-), Tiffany Renee 4/4/1978), Nathan Scott (7/29/1979-11/28/1979), Ethan (1981-), and Brandon Lee (10/?/1983-).

Paige Lenee (Friday, 11/11/1955-) married Taylor-grad Jay Alan Cunningham (10/12/1955-) on 12/31/77. They have two children: Kelsey Lenee (10/?/1974-) and Jameson. Paige showed the versatility as much as anyone. A National Merit Scholar, she graduated from Taylor with a major in musical composition and organ, and then went to Northwestern law school and became an attorney, at one time serving as general counsel for American United for Life, an anti-abortion group that sought to use legal means to overturn Roe v. Wade. Jay, a fine tenor who sang "In the Garden" at Mother's funeral, became a stockbroker.

Chuck

When Chuck was killed, he left three children aged 11, 9, and 2. That was the tragedy; God, in his mercy, redeemed it. Chuck had not been faithful in church attendance at the time of his death. But after his death, God provided an atmosphere in which the children at least were encouraged to go to church. And as adults, Richard became a minister and Greg was on Campus Crusade staff for several years. Richard Charles (Monday, 12/5/1949-) was born when Chuck and Billy lived just north of the home place, and I remember Chuck coming home and sitting on the side of the stove in the kitchen telling Mother and Daddy about it. Richard, who was named after Billy's late brother, married Diane Mary Bowen on 10/7/1972, graduated from St. Cloud and got his master's from Vanderbilt's Scarritt and became a Methodist pastor in Iowa. They have two children, Nathan Andrew (8/23/1976-), Timothy (5/?/1981-), and Jonathan David (4/10/1983-). Diane was a special education teacher.

Gregory Neil (Monday, 8/13/1951-) married Linda Kay Benson (10/4/1953) and they have three sons: Bryce Robert (8/4/1976-), Berent Charles 10/1/1980) (a reverse of his grandpa's name), and Brett Gregory (3/21/1983). Greg, whose arched eyebrows and mannerisms make him a clone of his father, graduated from the University of Minnesota in mathematics, served on Campus Crusade staff in West Chester, Pennsylvania., and San Bernardino, California. But lacking the support of home churches, his desire to go to Germany with

Campus Crusade was dashed, and he joined Hughes Aircraft and did classified work on submarines.

Both Linda and Diane got master's degrees. in special education.

Janet Sue (Sunday, 3/11/1958-) graduated from St. Cloud and became a social worker there in a half-way house for wayward girls. She is the perfect blend of her father and mother in her dark hair and smile. At the time of her father's death, Mother and Daddy said, Janet loved being with her dad and would go to the barn when he did the milking.

Paul

Paulette Kay (Tuesday, 11/6/1951-), an only child, was Job's Daughters honored queen in 1971 and later graduated from Kansas University (KU), winning the Richard Harkness Award, KU's highest broadcast award. She married fellow KU-grad Gregory Frank Cott (3/19/1951-) on 3/20/1976, and they have two sons, Stephen Paul (11/9/1978-) and Jeffrey Robert (8/10/1980-). The resemblance between these two brothers — Steve and Jeff — and their grandpa and uncle — Chuck and Paul is striking in the amount of difference in age, in the younger one's playfulness, even in their appearance. Paulette followed her father into broadcasting, in Topeka, in Sioux Falls at its main commercial station, KSOO, and eventually to South Dakota Public Radio.

P.S.

Our family became so scattered as we grew up, that rarely were two of us in the same community. In 1982 Dale Comstock moved to southern California where Greg Pippert already was living. Becky and I happened to be there at the time and got them together. I don't think Dale and Greg had seen each other in fifteen years. But they became close friends and both families went to Chuck Swindoll's church. It made me feel good — if Chuck and Lois couldn't be close, at least their children could. But when they did get together with their children, it may have been a little confusing — Bryce, Berent, Brett, Brent, and Bart. Then Marie's Gordie moved out to southern California but fortunately his sons were named Jordan and Taylor.

Chapter 7

We Younger Four

And finally, we younger four — Marie, I, Harriet, and Harold. Paul, of course, tells the story of our births. He said that every time Daddy came to where Chuck and Pauly were sleeping and said: "Boys, go to the barn for the rest of the night," he knew another baby was on the way. Indeed, the more Mother had, the faster they came. There were five years between Paul and Marie, four years between Marie and me, three years between me and Harriet, and two years between Harriet and Harold, who was born, by the way, when Mother was 45. Now for all that Mother and Daddy told us, these babies all came from heaven. I remember Mother remarking after Harold was born that he was her last — and I wondered how she could say that if heaven delivered the babies. This conversation, obviously, was before my graduate course in such matters at Portland 2. The children were spread out enough that I, like Marie's son Doug, couldn't quite keep track. Doug once remarked he didn't know whether Lois or Harold was the oldest, and he couldn't recall one of his aunt's names. One day, when I was a boy, Mother was mangling in her upstairs bedroom, and I told her I couldn't remember the seventh child in our family — Chuck, Pauly, Marie, me, Harriet and Harold, but who was the seventh? She said, "you know!" Now Mother and Daddy always playfully jousted, Mother often in the role of mentor, so I said, quite seriously, "Daddy?" Mother laughed and said, "No, not Daddy. Lois."

Actually, the times when all seven children lived at home at the same time were rare. Lois went off to Bible school when Harold was one, Chuck went to the Navy when Harold was three, and Paul left when he was five. So quite literally, we younger four were the only children at home during our early years, and, as a matter of fact,

Marie left for Bible school in 1948 when Harold was nine. Still, most of my memories were of us younger four going to Portland 2, to church, at home.

Marie

VaNita Marie was born on Thursday, July 3, 1930, Paul's fifth birthday. The middle child, Marie has always been happy and sweet and giving. Daddy adored her and teased her, calling her "Peggy O'Neill" and "our potato girl."

Marie, toddler

She carried Mother's burden after Mother's heart attacks, beginning in 1946 when she was a high school senior. Her home has been home to uncounted relatives, including me for five years, and others. None of the clan has the hospitality gifts that Marie has. None of the grandchildren, including my own children, have spent as much time in Iowa as Marie's children.

Like Lois and her braids, Marie had long curls that Mother brushed around her finger. Lois' braids got the scissors in St. Paul; Marie's curls, at 18. Daddy, who was very observant of facial characteristics, always remarked about her smile. She is Daddy's and Paul's match in telling stories, not jokes, but yarns and eccentricities about people we knew, always with an exact mimicry and gestures. She has worn glasses from the time she was two.

Marie, elementary school

Marie started school at Portland 6 while we were living on the Ladwig place. She finished at Portland 2, which she attended with me, with Miss Mullaney.

Marie, high school

My own view of Marie at the time during those early years was that she was a bit of a rascal. She liked to chew gum — and still does and cut up with Joan Toepher at church. Mother's heart attack in 1946 seemed to change that.

Marie, I felt, seemed to blame herself for Mother's illness. She became much more serious after that, still Marie, but more the Marie we all hold in such awesome regard today.

The war was on, and Marie was compelled to do something the rest of us had not done. She went to Nora Springs High School, not Mason City, and the folks' rationale was that Nora Springs had buses during wartime conditions of gasoline and tire rationing while Mason City did not. But she did fine at Nora Springs.

Marie, off to college

So, she rode the bus twice daily for four years with Mr. Bright, the Nora Springs druggist, at the wheel. Some of our neighbors were her classmates, Jake and Skunky Tevis and Bob Lindsay. I'm not aware how much she dated — for her eyes already were on Roy — but I do know that the class athlete and hunk, Leo O'Gorman, had his eyes on her, especially at the time of the senior prom in 1947.

She was the top typist in the class, a harbinger of what lay ahead for her professionally. She took piano lessons over the years, first with Aunt Esther and then with Mason City's best teacher, Ruth Swingen Brose. I remember riding along when Jim and Lois took her to New Hampton in 1947 to play in the contest. Her number was 'Malaguana'. When she graduated, she worked for Russ Cook who ran a grocery in a store near the viaduct on East State Street in Mason City and later in a Quonset hut near the Taylor Bridge on US 18. I'm sure Cook had a crush on her, and when she left he gave her an unqualified letter of recommendation.

Two of the central, determinative facts of Marie's life occurred about this time. First, she gave her heart to the Lord as a ?-year-old at a summer camp operated at Iowa Falls by the Rev. George Wolf of the American Sunday School Union. It was totally to be expected that after graduation from Nora Springs she would go on to St. Paul Bible Institute, and she did.

Second, she was in love with Jim's youngest brother, Roy. We all knew that this liaison was inevitable, almost from the time they met at Jim and Lois' wedding in 1943. Jim used to say that if anything happened to Lois, he would select Marie, a comment at which Marie scoffed, particularly since the Comstock she had was Roy. Roy had come to Mason City to visit.

Roy and Marie, St. Paul Bible Institute

He was tall and lanky, a basketball player at Claasen High School, a trombone player, devout, amiable, the thickest drawl any of us had ever heard, which made him the butt of countless jokes, mostly Pauly's, all of which he took with good nature. Roy joined the U.S. Army, playing with a service band at Fort Knox, Kentucky, where he had met a young lady named Millie. He, too, was headed for SPBI.

I'm sure those years were among the happiest and hardest of her life. The hard part was, of course, the Tieszen meddling into Glennis Wendt's life. The happiest was built around SPBI and her romance with Roy.

She and Roy had wound up at St. Paul in the fall of 1948. Marie was elected class vice president, and when the president dropped out of school shortly, she became class president. Roy, now a second-year student, had a reputation as one of the most spiritual-students at SPBI. Their romance quickened and moved toward engagement. It led Roy to make a trip to Mason City, and thereupon occurred one of our family's great stories.

Roy was determined to ask Daddy for Marie's hand in marriage. Now Daddy, not happy to lose one daughter, Lois, was even less happy at the prospect of losing another, Marie. Mother had a motherly sympathy for the young lovers' desire, and she and the rest of us were all holding our breath at what Daddy's reaction would be. At supper, to Mother's utter consternation, as Daddy sat eating silently, Pauly spilled the beans and through the entire meal he razzed Roy about his mission. By her own admission Mother "could have shook him." At any rate, after supper, Daddy and Roy went to the back porch and talked, and from what I was able to piece together, when Roy asked for them to be married right away, Daddy said in an understanding way that he preferred they wait a year but would not stand in their way. So, Roy and Marie waited a year. It was a wise decision. Daddy grew to hold Roy in great regard and affection.

Roy and Marie married in 1950 (and had their children in 1952, 1954, 1956, and 1958. "We did it all in the '50s," Marie said). Daddy walked Marie down the aisle at their 4 o'clock ceremony, Roy's sister Pearl and Billy stood with Marie, Chuck and Paul with Roy. Jim officiated.

Roy was manager of the appliance department at Montgomery Ward, and they lived in an upstairs apartment not far from the Alliance church the first autumn they were married. Then they joined Jim and Lois in Indiana, where Jim and Roy worked on degrees at Taylor.

Lilly Belle Dye Comstock, Roy, Marie, Magda, and
Harry, wedding day, 27 August 1950

Roy took a pastorate in Villa Park, a western Chicago suburb, then Oconomowoc, Wisconsin, in 1960, back to Wheaton where he began work on his master's degree. In the fall of 1961, I transferred from Pierre to Chicago. I went to spend the weekend with Marie — and wound up living with them for five years until 1966 when I moved to Washington.

Those were wonderful years for me. In the little house at 108 S Chase, Wheaton, the three adults had the two downstairs bedrooms, and upstairs, in the attic, were four little beds for Gordie, Gary, Dawn, and Dougie. Marie and I talked for hours and hours. The year 1961 was the one when Chuck was killed, and it seems now that that ordeal needed to be 'talked out' at length, and we did. Roy pastored the Missionary Church in Glen Ellyn and later a church at Lee Center, Illinois. One of the worst stunts I ever pulled in my life took place about this time. I had a new 1959 Wedgewood blue Buick LaSabre that I drove with a heavy foot. One time I took the boys and headed for Iowa. Gary, then about 7, was sitting in my lap (!) as I went roaring down the two-lane highway at

100 miles an hour. "Here, Gary, you take the wheel," I told him. And with Gary holding the wheel and a big semi bearing down on us, we went over a narrow bridge at the same time as the big truck. Only years later did Gary tell me that he had closed his eyes... Even now when I think of this, if I were Marie or Roy I'd grab me by the scruff of the neck...

It was a lively household — and when summer came the kids would split in different directions. Gordon went to Harold's farm four summers and parts of a third, Gary broke horses on a Colorado ranch, Dawn went to the Wheaton's Honeyrock summer camp in Wisconsin.

In 1964, I took leave from UPI and went to the Middle East. While I was away, Marie made a very significant decision. She went to Wheaton College in the thought that she might find work, in the dining hall or something. How wrong she was!

There was an opening in the Conservatory of Music, so she began there part-time. It was serendipity! It allowed her hidden talents to be unveiled and to flourish. And how they did! She became, in fact, the executive secretary for the dean of music, first the elegant, elderly Edward Cording and then for the rumpled creative genius, Harold Best. In effect, she became the associate dean. She not only ran their office for them, but she became the confidante for each of them, two totally different men in style and temperament. She sat in on the curriculum committee, the budget committee. I think it did for her what Cleminshaw did for Daddy. It demonstrated to her what she was capable of doing, how superior her ability was to some of the faculty Ph.D.s. I once remarked to Gary, "Have you ever thought what your mother, with an M.B.A. or a Ph.D. degree, might have accomplished professionally?" She might have outdone her children, which would have been no small accomplishment.

But even her professional accomplishments could not match her home-making and hospitality. She is organized: her towels, for instance, are folded just-so and stacked so that the corners match. She is more than Mother's match as a cook, and her apple pies and other pastries are absolutely awesome. Her butterhorn rolls are savored by all who have eaten Sunday dinner at 714 E Illinois, Wheaton, and there have been a few. As for hospitality, for instance, I came and stayed for five years. Look at it this way — her children left her home at the age of 22 or so; I, her brother, left her home at the age of 32! But I was not the last whom Marie and Roy took in. Nephew Larry came to live for a year or so at an important time in his life. Niece Paige lived there her senior year in high school and graduated from Wheaton Central. I once remarked to Daddy that if Marie didn't have someone to take care of, she would nab someone off the street. The feeling around the college was that the place to go in the evenings was the Comstocks.

Her family was known throughout Wheaton as model — brainy, believers, athletes, and sweet. The atmosphere in the home was – always — with guests or not, warm, gracious, sharing. But where the Comstock kids themselves went, often, was to Iowa and the farm. Gordie spent six or seven summers from his freshman year on with Harold. Dawn frequently went to stay with her grandparents, and Mother told how the three of them would sit on the roof of the front porch during the summer nights.

All of her brothers and sisters hold Marie as something precious and special. Harold and I were talking about something recently, and he commented to me, "For Marie, of all people, I would do anything."

WESLEY

I am the No. 5 child of seven. There is no question but that I have had and continue to have a varied and interesting life, for which I am grateful and which I in no way minimize. But the significance of what I have done and experienced shrinks when I think of my brothers and sisters. I do not have the peacemaking gift and warmth of Lois, the innately regal nature of Chuck, the wit and neighborliness of Paul. I do not of Harold. This isn't gratuitous self-effacement; it is merely a meager attempt to put into focus the traits I think are really valuable in life.

I was born in 1934 on May 13, Mother's Day that year and the same birthday as Joe Louis and Stevey Wonder. My middle name came from Gerald McKnight, husband of Mother's midwife. I am not sure that 'Wesley' came from John and Charles Wesley, although I became Methodist in later years. My nickname growing up was 'Bub', and I'm really sorry now it didn't stick. It surely beat 'Weasel', attached to me at the Alliance church by Roland Juhlin and others; I didn't figure out until recently it was an adaptation of my first name. My first four years were spent on the Ladwig place. I remember the outlines of the farm — the trees along the road, the stone columns of the house, the garage, and the barn. I vaguely remember how we kids set the curtains aflame in the upstairs bedroom and when a bull got loose in the barn. I distinctly remember the events of Sept. 19, 1936, when I challenged the ensilage cutter.

After we moved to the home place, I started Portland 2 and spent all eight years there. Miss Marjorie Mullaney was our teacher the first four years, and every day after the noon hour she would read aloud to us from a book. One time it was Mark Twain's *Tom Sawyer*. Years later, about 35 to be exact, when I met Becky I told her I was surprised she was not a blue-eyed blonde, but I did not know why I felt that way. A couple of years later, President Carter spent his vacation going down the Mississippi River on the Delta Queen river boat. I was along. We moored at Hannibal, Mo., where Twain wrote, and we dashed ashore. I went to a bookstore and picked up a copy of *Tom Sawyer* and began reading.

There it was: a couple of chapters into the book. A new girl is in town, Becky Thatcher, the daughter of the judge, with long yellow hair and blue eyes. In my subconscious I had associated blonde hair and blue eyes with the name Becky.

The best teacher I had at Portland 2 was Miss Margaret Quinn. She was excellent. We talked about issues. I told her that eventually, as people became more educated and aware, all countries would become democratic. It popped up on the next test. I did best of all in geography; in fact, in the state tests, I did my best and ranked with college graduates in map-readings.

Generally, Mother or Daddy would take Marie, me and Harriet or me, Harriet and Harold to school in the morning by car and we would walk the mile and a half home. Briefly we rode Silver, a frisky horse slightly larger than a Shetland, and tethered her in the horse barn. In the winter months, we would bring little jars with food in them that we would out on top of the stove in a pan of water to keep warm, or one of our parents would bring a hot lunch.

I have a strange, yet typical sensation about those first years in school. It regards time. It seemed to me at the time to be an interminable period; for instance, between the start of school at 9 and recess at 10:30. Or the same thing for any other similar time period. The springs and summers seemed to go on and on. I think of that summer after World War II, when Daddy had sugar beets that didn't get thinned. Now, in later years, the years absolutely speed by, faster and faster. I am not at all convinced that the measurements of time are absolute or remain the same. I loved our recesses at Portland 2. We played games. We played pum-pum-pull-away, and I remember Joan Behne even yet having to be pulled away. My own favorite was stealing sticks.

There were dark sides to country school. For one thing, there were 'sides'. So, often, without warning, one side would get 'mad' at the other side. One stretch, during my sixth or seventh grade, I was on the wrong side, and it absolutely devastated me. I would look forward to the evenings when Mother would have a special speaker or a visiting missionary out for supper (now I wonder, with guilt, how Richard Steeve, who lived with the Steils, handled it because he always was on the wrong side. I guess I know: he turned to crime). Miss Quinn had a game called 'English jail'. Every time we caught another pupil making an error in grammar — saying "ain't" being the most obvious — we could put their name on the blackboard in the English jail. We got out of jail by catching another student making a mistake. I managed to keep out of it most of the time, but guess who was in scores of times with no hope of ever getting out — Dick Steeve. During my third or fourth grade, the teacher — I can't remember whether it was Miss Mullaney or Miss Quinn — marked my report card as "annoys others." It also devastated me.

And I first bumped into death. Mark Behne, one of the four Behne kids who lived on the first farm to the west, died of a brain tumor. I had first heard the musical 'Oklahoma' at this time and I still think of him whenever I hear "...corn as high as an elephant's eye." About that same time, Jimmy O'Connor, a son-in-law of Mrs. Files at church, dropped dead of a heart attack after completing his run at Mason City Motor Coaches as a bus driver. I thought I was going to faint. In the summer of 1954, I was swimming at Clear Lake when a boy was caught under a raft that a lot of us had been playing on and he drowned.

I began to read — not the classics like Joyce said New York state required of its students, but baseball books by John Tunis and books like *T-Model Tommy* and others by Stephen W. Meader. It was one of those books that led to my creation of an elaborate fantasy network, built around sports and farming. I assembled a group of fellows who played all three sports (football, baseball and basketball) and had an elaborate farm near Mandan, North Dakota. One of my creations, whose name was taken from a book, was Hank Gorey, who played catcher, center, and fullback. Robert 'Bud' Robertson was a left-handed first baseman and forward. There were others, to my dismay, I no longer can remember. There were two brothers who operated a 640-acre, section-sized farm near Mandan, with mile-long stretches of corn, wheat, rye, millet (Daddy raised millet that year) pasture, and a herd of 50 dairy cows in equal numbers of Jersey, Holstein, Guernsey, and Brown Swiss. I created imaginary conversations, often spoken aloud until I was embarrassed to discover that someone was overhearing me. The very details of the fantasy revealed that at my core I was a generalist, not a specialist, and later as a wire service reporter, I was just that.

I often have said, as an adult, that the only ambition I ever had was to be centerfielder for the New York Yankees, and there was some truth in that. I simply am not a good athlete (although I did get to be a pretty fair volleyball player in the summers after finishing Iowa). Nephew Gordon, a crack basketball player, didn't get athletic genes from me.

But, oh, how I aspired to be. I shot thousands of corn cobs at the missing board over the door of the hog house, hitting maybe dozens. I threw thousands of corn cobs against the side of the barn in the general direction of squares marked off as strike, homerun, etc. But my favorite sport was football. By the time I was able to play, Chuck and Paul were home from the service. Paul threw bullet passes that stung when I tried to catch them.

Chuck threw his knee out several times kicking. A concomitant of that, I followed major league baseball religiously, starting with the St. Louis Browns Cards' 1945 World Series. Bob Feller, the Iowa farm boy turned Cleveland fireballer, was my favorite. The Indians and the Cincinnati Reds were my favorites on the strength of Mother's relatives in Cincinnati. I still know the Cleveland lineup for 1948 that won the pennant in a playoff with the Red Sox: Ed Robinson, 1b; Joe Gordon, 2b; Manager Lou Boudreau, ss; Ken Keltner, 3b; Dale Mitchell, who hit .300 every year and always led the league in triples), lf; Larry Doby, the first black in the American League, cf; Jim Hegan, c; and of course, Feller and Bob Lemon, the prize starters, and the incredible 'rookie' of the year, LeRoy 'Satchel' Paige, the ageless pitching legend of the Negro leagues. When I flew to Ohio to see Carol in the summer of 1953, we went to Cleveland and I saw Feller, in his waning years, warming up in the rightfield bullpen.

But my fantasy accompanied me every night as I did chores, including walking close to a half mile to the pasture after the cows. My chores each night were to do the chicken chores, that is, sprinkle them oats, check the water and the calcium shells, and gather the eggs; to fill the cob basket in the back porch; to feed and water the hogs (I generally carried two five-gallon buckets of water to that trough on the east side of the hog house, the one missing an end, while Daddy generally carried a 10-gallon can of water in each hand); and to throw down ensilage and hay for the cows. I started driving at 9 — my first experience was with the Model B going from the east 80 to the house, but Marie twitted me by saying the front bumper had come to rest against the fence. Later, in the summer of 1950, I broke my arm cranking the same 22-36 that had kicked against Paul's arm. I was unloading oats at Chuck's and either he or Billy took me to Park Hospital where Dr. J.C. Christopherson set the bone. This was the same troubled summer that Roy and Marie married.

And, politics, of course. It dates to Chuck and Paul's support for Wilkie. It was enhanced by a discussion I had with Jim as we were en route to New Hampton for Marie's piano contest solo. Jim said a government ought to balance its budget, just like families do. I agreed — at least for a few years. I remember writing a political essay on the wide-lined tablet at Portland 2 on prospects for the 1948 presidential race — and at 13 I was amazingly on target, Dewey, Warren, et al. I remember that as a senior in Mason City High School, I outargued the teacher on a political discussion. One Sunday night after church I hustled down to the Hanford Hotel just to shake hands with Republican National Chairman Guy Gabrielson. (Years later: Guy G. Gabrielson? Guy G. Gabrielson???)

I did a lot of work outside, but actually, my forte was cleaning house. Mother went to town on Saturday, promising to bring me something if I had cleaned. I always put it off, but by the time she came home during the afternoon, I had cleaned, vacuumed, dusted, swept under the beds, put away all the scraps and stuff. I am living proof that most — yes, most — men are tidier than their wives. And what Paul was to the John Deere cultivator (i.e., high speed), I was to the mangle. Could I iron (and still do)!

It was a burden for Mother and Daddy to send me to Mason City for my four years of high school. Marie, after all, had gone to Nora Springs. My going to Mason City meant that every day, week after week, year after year, they would have to improvise how to take and get me. In the fall of my ninth grade, Paul took me (and I was late frequently).

Throughout high school, often I would stay in town and wait at the Library. Never have I been so current as those years in reading so many magazines as *Life, Look, Colliers, Saturday Evening Post, Time, Newsweek, U.S. News, America.* Daddy would come by, and either honk or come in in his work clothes. We both were embarrassed, I'm sure.

My ninth grade was one of two or three of the hardest of my life. I transferred from Portland 2, with 10 students, to Roosevelt Junior High School, with close to 1,000. I flunked swimming two six weeks ("does not try"). I got a D in algebra. Worse, some of the farm kids who were my friends – Bob Krause, Chester Millard, Bob Wilson, and others — razzed me. I had had eczema on my hands for years. "Got the siff?" they'd chorus. "Pimp the simp," or worse, "Pimple simple," they would call me during the noon hour when we were eating together. I didn't like it. I have been in only two or three fights in my life — Russell Symes, Bob Klatt, Bob Wilson (I think an honest call would give me a 2-1 lifetime record). One day, I thought, I don't need to take this. So, I started buddying with some kids, actually of greater stature: Charles Wolf, now a big financier in New York and at Columbia University; Bob Horn, who worked at the library, now of Boston; others. A few weeks later, one of the old crowd came by and asked a bit sheepishly: "Where have you been?" What was immediately clear was that they hadn't meant to drive me away, that they were joking. But it was too late. Ironically, one of my old gang, Chester Millard, was elected senior class president at Mason City. "Who's he? I don't even know him!" groused Jean Engler, class valedictorian and later, I believe, vice chancellor at the University of Arizona.

But it was worth it. I had a good high school experience. My senior year was especially so: my brass quintet won a Division I in state; my debate team (I debated affirmative on "Resolved: the United Nations should be changed into a federal world government") went to state; I won the state high school sports writing contest. And I got a Merit Scholarship to the University of Iowa that paid my tuition of $180 a semester.

To pay my way through college, I got jobs each summer at the Decker's packing plant. The first summer, 1952, I worked every day in the by-products department, where all the condemned meat, bones, hair, and blood were cooked, dried, and ground up to sell as tankage. If packing-house workers are at the lower end of the hierarchy of laborers, the by-products was at the bottom of the hierarchy within the packing plant. It was hot — often up around 120 — and it stank. My straw boss was Bill Martin, an ancient black man whose daughter had her master's degree from Columbia, such achievement being a rarity then. One summer, I worked at home during the day, then wore my dirty clothes to Deckers for the evening shift, quickly went back into the work area where they could not see how dirty I was, and at the end of the day, threw my shirt and pants into the Decker laundry. I boasted that Mother did not wash a single shirt or pants for me that summer! The laundry man and janitor around the plant was Art Heinhold, a little man who went to the Free Methodist Church, and the father of Marilyn, a perky, pretty, young lady I dated a couple of summers.

Compared to my time in Mason City High School, my three-and-a-half years at the State University of Iowa were a breeze — and one of the happiest periods of my life. Academically, after competing with Jean Engler, Charles Wolf, Jean Marty, Socrates Pappajohn and others in Mason City, those freshmen were simply no match, and I rolled up sixteen hours of A (and two hours of C in physical education) as a first-semester freshman. When I graduated, I was class marshal by virtue of being the highest-ranking male in the College of Liberal Arts, although nine women were ahead of me. Talk about male chauvinism. And during my three-and-a-half years, I had missed not one football or basketball game or theater production.

My total B.A. degree, incidentally, cost $3,900. over my time in college, Mother and Daddy gave me $600 of that often, for instance, a load of oats I hauled to Portland and I paid that back within a year or two after I graduated. The rest of my degree I paid myself.

An altogether significant part of growing up was the devotions Mother would have with us four each night at our bedside. She would read and pray with us. One night I remember asking her repeatedly how one knew for sure that he was saved. She explained it was a matter of faith, and after I prayed, she told me that I had been saved. On my tenth birthday, we had dinner, a huge one typical of Mrs. Williams. There was a missionary at church. J. W. Mouw, I believe. He was an evangelist at all times, even during missionary convention, and he preached that way rather than tell missionary tales about the natives. I 'went forward' to the altar, and for a long time, I counted that day as the central one. When C.D. Tieszen was conducting evangelistic meetings at the Alliance church in 1950 a year before he came as pastor, I went forward again. He prayed with me (I remember his breath was bad, and I don't mean that sacrilegiously) and asked if I wanted to be "filled with the Holy Spirit." I said yes, but I had no idea what that meant, for it was years before the charismatic revival swept the country, and before my own systematic study of the Holy Spirit following a 1953 talk by Stanley Soltau (after a news conference at the University of Chicago during his America visit, Karl Barth remarked to me "That's it!" when I asked him whether a rediscovery of the Holy Spirit was the next big Reformation). But mostly, Mother's regular devotion and teaching and the consistency of her life, a structure that was fleshed out during my Inter-Varsity experience at Iowa that are responsible for my belief. My behavior was probably pretty good, certainly compared to Daryl Miller and Mac Dresbach at church, although I engaged in a certain amount of brinksmanship, stepping up to the very edge of misbehaving without being perceived as misbehaving. Furthermore, do you really think I would confess my sins in this book??

In a family in which I am proud to say our political beliefs run the gamut, I am a liberal if not a radical. I have, for instance, always been acutely aware of racial injustice. How did this happen? One contributing factor occurred during that rough freshman year at Roosevelt Junior High. I was taking my lumps as a farm kid, unable to cope with it very well, and a fellow sitting next to me in Miss Cooke's European history class was Dick Macer, a black and a football player. I was friendly to him, feeling he also was something of a target, and he was friendly to me. It just picked up momentum. I think it also helped that the premiere athlete ever to graduate from Mason City High School was Bernard Bennett, a black senior when I was a freshman. At the University of Iowa, I was proud that the Student Christian Council's Mary in the campus-wide Christmas program in 1954 was played by a black woman, Barbara Oliver. And classy Bill Martin was my straw boss at Deckers. I handpicked my successor as president of the Inter-Varsity chapter, Sam Ling, a Chinese student from Taiwan. IV was one of the first organizations on campus to have an international student as president. With United Press in South Dakota, I became very aware of the plight of the Sioux Indians, among the poorest people in America, and I wrote stories about them. I tried to hire Jim McCord in Sioux Falls; he would have been the first black journalist to work for UP. I got turned down (and should have quit). These things all happened in the 1950s, years before the civil rights revolution really exploded. It all climaxed when Daddy's physician at Mayo Clinic in 1973 was a 26-year-old black internist, Dr. Stephenie Lucas. Later, her father, former Wayne County (Detroit) Sheriff William Lucas, whose nomination to be U.S. assistant attorney general ran into such controversy, and I were Fellows together at Harvard. But what gave me a sound rationale for these feelings were my Old Testament classes at Wheaton Graduate School. One cannot study the prophets without becoming radicalized about the plight of the poor and the oppressed.

I never yearned to be married, and my family never put any pressure on me (or maybe I just didn't catch it). When Becky Manley phoned the White House March 10, 1977, for me to speak at a conference in Oregon, and when we talked again a few days later, I knew this was different. In May we had our first evening together in Marshalltown, Iowa, and later on that night Mother, now alone on the farm, served tea and Becky and I walked the yards in the wee hours. We both said later that we knew from the beginning this was it. We married a year and a day from the first telephone call. I have never met anyone anywhere with the people skills — both 1:1 and to a group — as Becky, and she really is about the only authentic evangelist I know. My colleagues — pagan or not — adore her. Elizabeth Marie (after her Aunt Marie and several grandmas) was born in Jerusalem January 24, 1985, the day the Naqoura peace talks broke down in Lebanon (I worked that day), and David Manley was born on Boston's North Shore November 29, 1986. Last Sunday I happened to be at church alone with the kids. It was stewardship Sunday and all of us, with the Sunday School children leading the way, moved forward silently to take our pledges to the altar while the choir sang. I was in my accustomed center-aisle seat. All of a sudden Elizabeth, walking down the aisle with her class, spotted me. She grabbed me as she was passing and gave me a quick kiss. The people in my section gave a quiet cheer and one man whom I didn't know reached over and touched me on the shoulder. "You're the luckiest man in town," he said. "I surely am," I said. My ecstasy was momentary. David walked by, holding the hand of his teacher, and I slunk in the seat so he wouldn't see me. A few moments later, at a particularly soft portion of the choir's motet, I heard this very familiar voice coming down from the altar say: "Where are we going??" and then, "WHERE'S MY DADDY???" The man I didn't know did me the favor of not saying a word.

Harriet

Harriet's tragedy is that she never had a chance. Almost from the beginning her frail body had three strikes against it.

Harriet didn't actually become 'Harriet' until she was several years old. She was born Alma Harriet Pippert, after Mother's late older sister, Alma, on Thursday, March 18, 1937. Chuck always called her 'Alma'. It was in the midst of the Ladwig mess and six months after my accident. Mother said she was a 'blue' baby, meaning, I think, that Harriet was premature.

She was frail. Her first teeth all went bad. She started school at Portland 2, and we were aware enough of her poor health that I, then all of 9, worried that she wouldn't be promoted. But she was.

Mother and Daddy bought her a rather fancy tricycle, purple, with a running board for others to stand on the back, with a bell attached to the steering bar.

Two or three things happened when she was a little girl that wrench me when I think of them. When we still had the windmill, Daddy had crawled up to the platform, around 40 feet up. Harriet, just a tot, was standing directly below. Daddy dropped a brace and bit and the knob struck her on the side of the face. On another occasion, we had eaten Sunday dinner with the Walter Williams and spent the afternoon with them. Either just before the evening service or during it, Harriet wandered off and got lost. No one knew where she was. Walter Williams, leading songs, asked if anyone had seen her. During the sermon, Mrs. Williams, her piano-playing responsibilities done, got in their Ford along with me, and I think Marie, and went searching the streets. There I saw Harriet, picking her out by her white high-top overshoes, walking slowly, aimlessly on the sidewalk. We had sung a hymn in church that evening that I never hear to this day without its reminding me of Harriet getting lost:

> 'Twas a glad day when Jesus found me,
> When His strong arms were thrown around me...

Another time, Harriet and I were invited to a birthday party for Marlin Tevis. We were playing group games, and somehow Harriet didn't get the hang of it. Marlin said: "Oh, she's dumb." A few moments Harriet came over to where I was sitting and then I noticed she was crying. She had heard him.

About this time, several youngsters in our acquaintance, Phyllis Kellogg and others, came down with rheumatic fever, a disease that left one down for several weeks with the dark possibility of permanent heart damage. Harriet was diagnosed as having rheumatic fever in the fall of her fourth year. "Oh!" I felt. "Imagine having to spend three or four months in bed." Little did we know. Instead of three or four months, she would never recover from the effects of rheumatic fever or the emotional trauma it caused her.

Often, she was sick and would spend two or three weeks in Park Hospital under the care of Dr. G.K. Sartor and later Dr. Van Hunt. It finally was determined that the cause of her illness was· bad tonsils draining poison into her system. She spent one month in the hospital just to have those tonsils taken out, and even then her illness continued. This was before the days of health insurance, and Daddy paid the entire bill. Another time Daddy had gotten his check from Portland for his entire bean crop, taken it to Mason City, and turned over the whole thing to Park Hospital.

For long stretches Harriet's pulse raced between 120 and 140 and her temperature stayed between 100 and 103. One time, while I was at the University of Iowa, Mother wrote: "I'm at a loss…" Later, Mother wrote: "I have a faith that doesn't waver in her behalf." And sometime later, Mother wrote: "Well, we don't always understand why the tests we have to go thru with, but this we do know 'God leads His dear children along, some thru the fire, some thru the flood, but *all* thru the *Blood*. I'm sure God has a purpose for it all, and wants to refine us, as silver, and take out all the dross, and bring us out vessels pleasing unto Himself.

Even though this has brought some tears, it has also brought deeper consecration on my part. Pray for Harriet that she will know Him better. It will take some praying for the finances also."

But Harriet was never to recover.

Mother, Marie, Lois, Harriet

From the fourth grade through high school, Harriet spent part or most of every school year at home, with tutors. She spent most of her waking hours in a special chair that would tilt back.

Mother often put it under an apricot tree that had sprung up from a pit outside the east side of the back porch; Harriet watched it grow to full height. She was a dear Christian girl. She obviously had few friends her age; Mother did the best she could for her. She took her to California to see Grandpa Halsor in 1949 and 1950 and to see Lois in Atlanta in 1954.

Mother invited women to the house for tea and to talk with Harriet. Aunt Esther helped her get scrapbooks started. Norleda Sandy tutored her through her final grade school years, but generally spent more time sipping tea and eating ginger creams than actually tutoring Harriet. She graduated from Nora Springs High School in 1956.

The one thing that Harriet could do par excellence was play the piano. She had a few lessons from Aunt Esther and some from Ruth Swingen Brose, supposedly Mason City's best. She could play the piano in a way that took no energy and put no pressure on her heart. So she played by the hours. Good songs – 'Rustles of Spring', Mother's favorite, and especially hymns. How she could play hymns! Years later, with the worst effects of her illness now obvious, she would play hymns with skill and grace notes.

After graduating from Nora Springs High School, she went off to St. Paul Bible Institute. It was a calculated risk on Mother and Daddy's part, but we felt this would be the right atmosphere for her and one in which she could make friends and get some social experiences in a non-threatening atmosphere. The year, I think, went well. But that summer, we all went to Oconomowoc, Wisconsin, to visit Marie.

Mother was concerned. Harriet was crying for no apparent reason, and she remarked to Mother: "Something terrible is happening to me." It was. She had an emotional break from which she never recovered. The diagnosis proved to be schizophrenia. It was to be far worse than the ravages of the rheumatic fever. What was the cause of the mental problems? It was Mother's belief that all those years of high temperatures literally burned her brain and all those years of a high pulse weakened her physical ability to withstand, a belief that Harriet's doctors have never challenged. Mother eventually had to sign papers in effect committing her.

Harriet spent time in St. Joseph's Mercy Hospital, getting shock treatment. She underwent a thorough examination at University Hospitals in Iowa City in early 1958 and finally was transferred to Independence State Hospital. She was home for a while that year but finally asked to be taken back when she realized she couldn't cope. Mother would make the drive to Independence to see her every week or two. Nothing helped. Her medical records were several inches thick. Finally, she was transferred to the Cerro Gordo County Home on US 18 west of Mason city, and there she was for years.

For a while, Uncle Carl would visit her and take her riding; in fact, he and Aunt Esther took Harriet to Chuck's funeral in 1961. Meanwhile, the cost of Harriet's care was beginning to worry Daddy. So, in August 1962, Paul and I made a deal with J.C. Dickinson, a member of the Cerro Gordo County Board of Supervisors, that in exchange for $4,000 and a monthly payment of $50 a month, the board would write off Harriet's bill of then $7,000 or $8,000. Implicit in the deal was the understanding that Harriet's disabled Social Security payments would be turned over to the state to more than meet the monthly payment of $50 or $100.

In 1988, Cerro Gordo County transferred her to the Cherokee (Iowa) State Hospital. While there, she broke her leg, a fracture that the hospital's psychiatrist could not explain. Since Cerro Gordo County did not have full-time nursing care, Harriet was transferred first to Manly's health care center and then to Tecumseh, Nebraska. I bought her share of the farm in court-approved transactions, but sadly, most of it was eaten up by lawyer's fees.

Harriet changed. Instead of the sweet, polite little girl, she became bigger than life, almost tyrannical in the way she treated other patients and staff. She chain-smoked. If it were not so tragic it would be funny, for she would light a cigarette and take so deep a drag that it left half the cigarette in ash. Her expressions were overdrawn. She laughed too loud. But no matter how long any of us had been away, she always recognized us and called us by name and welcomed us graciously.

And she played the hymns; oh! how she played. I have a hunch that when the saints gather in heaven to sing hymns, Harriet will be their accompanist.

HAROLD

Mother had wanted to name Harold, rather, 'David Elthan'. 'Elthan' was Paul E. Freligh's middle name, and it was similar to the name of, I think, a former boyfriend, Leo Elthon, who became governor of Iowa in the mid-1950s. She chose 'Harold' ultimately because it was a variation of 'Harry'. I have always been sorry that Harold wasn't named David, for he reminds me so much of the biblical David: fair, strong, winsome. Harold was the youngest of the seven, born when Mother was 45, on Tuesday, November 28, 1939, in the same house in which Daddy was born. Harold began farming at the age of 7, quite literally. Even at his age now — he turns 50 in three days — no one has farmed our home place longer. His experience in farming that land is much longer than Daddy's on the same plot. I once asked Daddy which one of us four boys was the best farmer (being quite certain he wouldn't say me). "Harold," he said. But that in no way describes the full measure of who Harold is.

When Daddy died in 1976, Mother said that in twenty years of their working together she never had heard one cross word exchanged between Daddy and Harold. It was Harold who cared gently for Mother in her last years and held her as she passed from this earth.

This opens a small window into the depth and breadth of his character.

Becky says that rarely has she met anyone with Harold's perception and curiosity about people and life. Whenever I speak with him by phone, he asks me political questions. Dr. Stephenie Lucas adored Harold and said she had never met a white person so clear of racism as he is. A Wheaton College faculty member once told me that part of Gordie's drive stemmed from his six or seven summers with his Uncle Harold. In the same manner as Roy and his boys, I doubt that Harold has missed more than one or two games and events in which his children have participated.

Harriet, Harold, and I went to Portland 2 together. After the philandering of the previous kids, Bob Klatt, now a mechanic at Northwest Airlines in Minneapolis, and I covenanted to keep such naughty information from being passed on to our younger sisters (Mary Klatt and Harriet) and brother (Harold). So I remember those days as being pretty placid. Mother was of the opinion that Norleda Sandy, the teacher, paid much more attention to Donita Emmert and Odette Hanson than to Harold. Even as a little boy, he had wide interests. He picked wild blackberries along the road and made jam himself. "The boy with a smile," Mother called him.

Harold, like Paul before him, was not very big as a boy. Pauly cut up with him a lot. One noon day, Harold was crawling up on the ledge of the screen in the back porch when he tumbled and his head hit the cement floor. "He's out!" Pauly exclaimed.

Mother rushed him to Dr. Henley in Nora Springs, who told her to keep a close watch on him all afternoon. So Mother held him all afternoon under the apricot tree until, towards evening, he regained awareness. Mother and Daddy used to speak of Pauly's obvious agony at what had happened.

In 1947, Daddy took his job with Cleminshaw and Chuck was preparing to move onto his own place. Harold simply took over. Mother saved a wonderful note penciled on notebook paper: "Mother. I am out runing (sic) the corn binder. Harold." Mother dated it September 3, 1948. Harold was 8 years of age. I came home from Roosevelt Junior High one day to see him out plowing west of the house with Chuck's Oliver 70, his head barely showing above the steering wheel, his foot barely able to reach the clutch. Both times he hooked up the tractor himself.

Harold, in 1953, was among the last to graduate from Portland 2, where Mother had taught nearly 40 years earlier. In Mason City, he played the French horn. He was still slight, but strong. He was the top wrestler at his weight in his gym classes all three years, and he acknowledged later he wished he could have wrestled competitively. He also was gifted with his hands — "His fingers can make anything run," Mother used to say — and like Chuck and Paul before him, he made bookcases and other things in his classes. He graduated in 1957. During those years I got more active in the young people's group at the Alliance church. This would have been in 1950 and following, or when Harriet was 13 and Harold 11. Mother urged me to take them along to volleyball or whatever was going on. I would take Tracy Kinsel or Al Uthoff home and we would sit in the car and talk, while Harriet and Harold sat quietly in the back seat, listening with wide ears, I'm sure, to our conversation about girls and the birds and the bees. Harold grew to be as active in the young people's group.

He sang in a quartet for a while. But it was his misfortune to have been a teen-ager and young adult at the Alliance church when C.O. Tieszen, not Lowell Young, was pastor.

There is a versatility to Harold and an ability to grow. In 1955, at age 15, he started taking piano lessons from Mrs. Hall. He took up the bow and arrow. He served in the U.S. Army in 1962, the third of us brothers to spend time in the service, and he said later he regretted he didn't serve longer. He served at Fort Carson, Colorado, and Fort Lewis, Arkansas. In 1965 he became a hog buyer for Armour, a professional position.

He became president of the Oriental Missionary Society's Men for Mission group. In 1971, he went on a Men for Mission short-term mission project to Colombia. Others included Lloyd Stevens, Wendell's father and a close friend of Harold; Wayne Foell, the 'mayor' of Portland; Jim Egner; Clifford Foell; and Rolland Wike. Their project was to build a church. He shipped down his bulldozer, and Lois, who was there, said later that during the siesta when everyone else was relaxing, Harold was out running his bulldozer.

"I'll go back again," Harold told the Mason City Globe-Gazette. And he did, next time to dirt-poor Haiti. If Marie and Roy were inevitable, so, to me, were Harold and Sandy Ballhagen. Sandy was an excellent soprano soloist — and pleasant and pretty as well. She attended the Alliance church, too. Her parents farmed near Rockwell and had been good friends of Aunt Bella and Uncle Shirley. Her mother was an absolutely fastidious housekeeper; her father was a very funny man who looked like Telly Savalas and loved to "go ridin" on his "sickle," or motorcycle. When they first began to date, Paul and I happened to be home, so we went with Harold to help Ballhagens make hay. "Paul and Wesley, why don't you go up in the haymow and stack bales," Mr. Ballhagen said. "Harold, maybe you can go out in the field and help Sandy rake." Pretty clear whom he was currying, Paul and I getting the toughest jobs in making hay and Harold the pleasant little task of raking — and helping Sandy at that.

His and Sandy's first farm was near Rockwell, then they bought the old Files place from Dean Huff just south of Portland in 1969, and it became their home place. His yards were like you would expect — impeccable. He set out more groves and built two big steel sheds. Uncle Jess was showing Mr. Ballhagen his steel shed, and Mr. Ballhagen replied brightly: "That's really nice, Jess, except Harold has two." When they walked inside, Mr. Ballhagen rubbed it in and said, "Harold's have concrete floors." I used to say that every time I came home Harold had another new machine that I had never operated.

His leadership in the neighborhood grew. He was elected president of the Midland Cooperative and later became the first Pippert on the board of the Portland Cooperative Co., from 1983-1989. He ran for the Nora Springs school board — and lost to a woman candidate. The children came: Annette Marie, Tuesday, July 4, 1968; Heather Rae, Sunday, September 21, 1969, two days before her Grandpa Pippert's birthday; Jason Harold, December 29, 1972, Jennifer, August 11, 1975. Like their cousins, they were super-achievers. Annette majored in statistics and chemistry at Iowa State; Heather was Miss Nora Springs in the 1988 North Iowa Band Festival and went on to North Iowa Area Community College and then the University of Iowa. Jason showed flair as an artist and designer and played varsity basketball and football, going both ways as running back and linebacker, but even his ability did not match his essential sweetness or 'magic'. Jennifer showed spiritual sensitivity. And Sandy grew, taking a job as a teacher's aide at the Gerard school for emotionally disturbed children in the old MacNider mansion, then going on to get her degree in special education from Buena Vista in 1987 and returning to Gerard as teacher. Last but not least, in 1987 she became lay pastor of her home Rockwell Congregational Church.

There is in Harold a fundamental sweetness wrapped in a certain reserve. It is not immediately apparent, but he has a gregariousness equaling anyone in the family. He likes to meet people and talk — far more than, for instance, I do. The sweetness also masks a confidence in his own ability. Intelligence he has, no question. If only he reduced more to account books than simply tucking away in his fertile brain! He knows who he is and what he wants to do. Surely some of this stems from having made his own way since he was 7 or 8. Most importantly, I know of no one who has followed more faithfully the commandment to honor thy father and mother, and this is surely a key reason why Harold's own children revere him. Gradually the routine had set in during the late 1960s and early 1970s. Daddy did less and less farm work, but still was frequently on the big International that Harold got. Daddy had consummate respect for Harold's prowess as a farmer, and Harold was respectful in return. That led to Mother's remark at the funeral home after Daddy's death that she had never heard a cross word between them.

These acts of honor were carried by Harold to a wondrous, beautiful conclusion in his care for Mother during the final years of her life. Mother stayed on the farm alone after Daddy's death in 1976 until 1979. Then she moved to the Manor, formerly the Hanford Hotel, and then, after a bad fall, she went into the Americana nursing home in Mason City as her mind and body slipped. Despite a heavy load as a farmer and a father, Harold went to the Americana each meal to feed her. The end came close to noon on April 8, 1983, with Marie; Gary, Karen and Krista; Becky and I; and Harold in the room. It was clear death was at hand. Mother lay in a coma. The Bible was read and prayers were offered. Then, suddenly, she became alert, her eyes open and full of fright, and sat up in bed. Harold quietly told her to open her mouth so she could breathe more easily, and she did, an expression of calm coming over her face. And as her last-born held her, she passed away. Marie said later that when Mother opened her eyes, it was Jesus she saw.

Epilogue

Marie

Marie's three boys graduated from Wheaton and her daughter from Taylor. Gordon (3/18/1952-), in Gary's view, would have been an all-conference basketball player at Wheaton if he had one more year of eligibility. Instead, he married Miss USA, Karen Morrison of Illinois, got his master's degree from Northwestern's Kellogg business school and became vice president for program for MAP International and traveled the globe. They have three children — Jordan Morrison (3/15/1982-), Taylor Lee (4/15/1985-) and Whitney Yoo Jung (8/31/1989-). Gary (2/23/54-) married Wheaton-grad Karen Werner of Fourth Presbyterian church in Washington, got his Ph.D. from top-rated University of Chicago, and quickly published bundles as a tenured philosopher at Iowa State while Karen got as many credits as an accomplished actress. They have two children — Krista Marie (11/17/1982-) and Benjamin Dhruva Werner (11/31/1984-). Dawn Marie (2/24/1956-) got her degree in psychology from Taylor (graduating with money in the bank), then a nursing degree from Chicago's Rush Hospital, eventually joined a pharmaceutical house and traveled widely. With an M.B.A. and her intuitive business sense, she probably would have owned it. Doug (6/24/1958-) was the family darling. He got his degree in religious studies, married Emily Stewart Goyer in Dallas, worked for Ross Perot's EDS in Dallas for nearly ten years and they have two children, Austin Wesley (8/8/1986-) and Reid Stewart (6/20/1988-).

Wesley

Elizabeth Marie (1/24/1985-) was born in Jerusalem, a curly-haired blonde with brown eyes, and David Manley (11/29/1986-) was born in Boston, a curly-haired blonde with blue eyes. Elizabeth's favorite store: Hechinger's lumber yard and hardware store! At 4 she told her mother how to repair the vacuum cleaner and may prove to be the mechanic I wasn't. Move over, Chuck, Paul, and Harold! Elizabeth is my surrogate.

When David was born, for his birth announcement I excerpted I Samuel 21: "Is not this David of whom they sing and dance?" It was a prophecy come true. My son.

Harold

After Mother died, Harold fought to keep the farm in the family. He persuaded his brothers and sister to help buy the adjoining long-sought 80 acres on the north end of the home place. Then he performed an architectural marvel on the barn by cutting huge doors in the front of it so that he could put big machinery in it.

His children followed in his tracks: Annette Marie (7/4/1967-) graduated almost at the top of her class at Nora Springs and majored in chemical statistics (whew!) at Iowa State. When she was a ninth grader, she came to Washington to visit and went to a White House party where Carter's chief of staff Hamilton Jordan saw her and started making a pass!

Heather Rae (9/21/1969-) was Miss Nora Springs-Rock Falls in the 1988 North Iowa Band Festival, and went on to North Iowa Area Community College on a scholarship and then the University of Iowa. Jason Harold (12/29/1972-)

played all sports, drew exquisite drawings (one of which hangs in David's bedroom), played in the band, worried about his Dad's crops, but mostly, had a certain magic. Jennifer (8/11/1975-) was the equal of her older brothers and sisters, a spiritually sensitive young lady. I told Marie, "Harold's four may be gaining on your four!"

Chapter 8

Life Together

California

Seeking their fortune, Mother and Daddy headed to California in 1922 or 1923. They lived in Orange County, near the site of Crystal Cathedral in Garden Grove. Daddy worked in the orange groves and pepper fields near the town of Talbert.

Japanese workers told him that Japan would whip the world in ten years — a prophecy that almost came true at the time of Pearl Harbor and has come even closer true economically in the 1970s and 1980s. Mother went to hear the evangelist Amy Semple McPherson. On the good side, Chuck was born on March 29, 1924, and Paul on July 3, 1925, in Talbert with Dr. C.C. Violet helping with the births.

But the hard times continued. The house burned, apparently to the ground, and Mother lost all of their wedding presents and things from her own home. The crop failed. Relatives on both sides had followed them to California, often staying with them. Finally, in 1927, they headed back east. Chuck and Paul are among the few people in the United States who were born in California but moved east. Millions did it the other way around. Paul remembers the trip back took many days in the Dodge, its wind vents wide open. He also remembers that the folks stopped to get him some lemon drops, which were about the best thing he had ever had.

Back to Iowa

Back in Iowa, the Folks moved frequently the first few years. They went first to the Gage place, little more than a big garage along the Winnebago River between the Taylor Bridge and Portland. Paul, still a tyke, remembers crossing the river with the Pippert uncles.

Then it was to the Krieger place (Mother always called it the Felt place), on the northwest edge of Portland and three-quarters of a mile south of Grandpa and Grandma Pippert on old US 18. The house and barn were on opposite sides of the road, and here Chuck and Pauly tried out those cigarettes and here Pauly burned down the bean crop. At the time of Mother's funeral in 1983, Lois, Paul, Marie, Harold, and I drove by it and Paul, Harold, and I did so in 1988. Now the house is about ready to collapse, and Ben Curran's cattle roam through the yards.

From there, the folks moved to the Ellis place a mile and a half south of Emory, a switching place for the Mason City & Clear Lake streetcar. Here Marie was born July 3, 1930, five years to the day after Paul.

The Ladwig Place

On January 1, 1931 — in those days moving day was January 1 — the Folks moved to the Ladwig place a mile east of Portland along the Milwaukee railroad tracks. I was born there on Mother's Day, May 13, 1934, and Alma Harriet, March 18, 1937. Mother and Daddy lived on the Ladwig place about seven years, longer than anywhere else except for the home place where they moved in 1939.

The Ladwig place was the scene of some of the richest lore in the family. It was located on a gravel road along the Milwaukee railroad tracks one mile east of Portland and a quarter mile north, or a quarter mile west and one mile south of what became the home place. The house had squat columns of stone, and the barn was typically broad-hipped. A single-car garage set alongside the driveway, and there Rev. Lorentzen, the traveling evangelist, and his family lived for a while.

The Ladwig lore: one Sunday night Daddy saw a car bearing Indiana license plates that was parked on the gravel road only a block or two from the farm. It was loaded with men. Daddy was pretty sharp about noticing things, and it bothered him. Daddy drove around the block and finally cancelled going to church. Finally it went speeding away. The next day we learned that the Dillinger gang had robbed the First National Bank in Mason City. Meanwhile, Uncle Al spent the night at the bank counting money.

That was nowhere near the most gripping tale, however. The *real* story began decades earlier with the Ladwig twins, Rufus and Ruel, members of a fine, upright, church-going family who lived on old US18 on what we knew as the Bartlett farm when we were growing up. Despite their fine reputation and character, both twins committed suicide.

They had a cousin named Charley Ladwig, and Charley lived on the Ladwig place with his wife and son Ed, a dark, shifty sort who was good with gadgets. In the upstairs bedroom, Charley died, and the next morning the sheriff ruled that Charley, too, had died a suicide. He had done it by taking Paris green. Doc Henley swore, however, that it was not a suicide at all — that there was Paris green in Charley's stomach but no trace of it in his mouth. Everybody assumed that Ed had used a tire pump to push Paris green through his dad's mouth into his stomach. Daddy believed it. And he said Doc Henley insisted that was what happened to his dying day. But it stayed on the books as a suicide.

A few months later, Mother and Daddy moved onto the Ladwig farm. Charley's widow, meanwhile, married a man named Rodman. Ed continued to get stranger and stranger and mosey around the farm. More than once, Daddy bundled up the brood and drove around the block or went to the grandparents because he sensed Ed Ladwig was hovering somewhere. "Old Ed was lurking everywhere," Paul recalls. Sometimes the folks would find chickens which should have been roosting, scattered in a field at night — a sign that something had disturbed them — and the next day there would appear to be fewer fowl in the coop.

Once something happened that made Mother laugh every time she told it. In the middle of the night on the Ladwig place, Mother heard a noise and thought she saw the silhouette of a man in the hallway. She told Daddy, who by this time had put on several scores of pounds from the tall, lanky man he was at the time he got married, got up and edged into the hallway. There he saw the man, too, and took a mighty swing at him. A pair of long underwear that was hanging in the hallway to dry went flying through the air. What Mother had heard was the underwear flapping in the breeze and what she saw was the silhouette created by the full moon shining behind the longjohns.

But there was little levity with the Ladwigs. Ed finally was adjudged insane and sent to the Independence state hospital. He had married Maude Cannon, a genial, heavy-set woman, who sued for divorce. She lived in mortal fear that Ed would escape and kill her, too. One afternoon in September 1936, Mother and Daddy were in Charles City testifying as character witnesses in the divorce suit, and we kids were home playing. Chuck and Pauly were turning the fly wheel on an ensilage cutter beside the garage when I, 2 years 4 months, toddled up unawares and stuck my hand in the open gears. Lois took me to the road, hailed a passing car — I don't know to this day who it was — and took me to Dr. Henley in Nora Springs, and then he took me to Mercy Hospital in Mason City where he amputated the fingers. Far worse, during the tense months that followed with Ed's sanity in question, Mother was pregnant. Harriet was born a blue baby with a difficult infancy. It is Harriet, in all likelihood, who is paying the price for the Ladwig lunacy.

Eventually Ed was released, remarried, and lived in Rockford. Years later, when we were living on the home place, we got word that Ed Ladwig had committed suicide by hanging himself. Mother remarked that although she never thought she would say that about anyone, she was glad he was dead. Daddy had some interesting things to say. Ed Ladwig, he said, was the best landlord he ever had, and for instance, if Daddy or Mother wanted something, he always got it for them. The real bastard was Rodman, who during the depression and drought of the mid-1930s, tried to foreclose Daddy.

In addition to the Ladwig place, Daddy also farmed the '110', a piece of land just north of the farm along US 18. It was owned by Rev. A.B. Swan, who also owned the '80' that Uncle Calvin farmed north of the home place. Daddy never bought either parcel, although he probably should have.

The Home Place

Home is on the crest of a small hill — its many, many secrets hidden in the ageless house and barn, the vestiges of Mother's flowers still peeking out in the backyard and a massive grapevine forming a natural arch. But not all of its secrets. The first night I ever spent with Becky, as we walked in the front yard I told her that the house still looked drawn with grief for its oldest and longest tenant who had departed six months earlier — Daddy, who was born in it in 1897 and who was living there when he died 79 years later.

The farm had been in the Pippert family for generations — it was known, in fact, as the Old J.H. Pippert farm, for Great-Grandpa Pippert — and Daddy and several if not all of his brothers and sisters were born there. But it had been sold, rented out, and finally re-purchased from Great-Grandpa Pippert's estate in 1938 by Daddy and Mother.

The farm is the Northwest 1/4 of Section 9 of Township 96N of Range 19W. To the north was Uncle Calvin's 80 (Chuck and Billy's first home in the late 1940s was directly one mile north); to the east was Pete Steil's place. A gravel road went east-west on the south side of the farm. To the east rows of Steils' trees lined both sides of the road, aesthetic, although every time a storm knocked down a limb it fell on a power line and we lost our electricity. The trees fell to the buzz saw when the road was widened in 1958-1959 and the grade was paved to create new US 18.

(When nephew Doug left Dallas and the hi-tech world in 1989, he considered agriculture and the place that caught his eye was the old Steil place, now owned by Gary Howell, former Federal Land Bank tyrant.)

Along the west side of the 160 ran an ungraded road that was little more than a trail. Dick Steeve, Marie and I used to watch the melting snow run under a bridge about a quarter of a mile to the north. After it was graded, in about 1940, lovers used to park under a lone tree about three-quarters of a mile north. Occasionally, a car was parked there, and Marie and I were scared to death. Once I was so scared that I finally walked a quarter mile east, then south through the fields. The original building site was actually a bit to the west and north of the grove, and when I first worked that field, I would see bits of broken dishes in the soil.

The farm is on the north side of the road. The driveway is at the crest of a small hill, which always made turning into it a bit dangerous — for one can't see the oncoming cars until just before the turn and tailgaters compound the peril. Daddy used to deal with the turn by pulling into the left-hand lane to avoid the tailgaters, even though he could not see oncoming traffic with which he could have had a head-on accident! Mother was nearly killed in 1973 when she braked to make the turn into the driveway and a tailgater hit her car and sent it like croquet ball into the ditch and an adjoining field. It was the last she ever drove.

Along the short driveway, three big box elder trees, now gone, were to the west; two smaller box elders were set back aways to the east. To the west was the house, farther to the west was the weathered, unpainted combination woodshed-shop-utility room. Directly ahead of the driveway, slightly to the west, were the windmill and milk house, and slightly to the east, was the barn, a big A-shaped structure with a lean-to horse-barn on its east side. We used to jump off a ledge high in the north end of the barn and ride a bag swing all the way to the big barn door on the south side. It was a marvelous experience. But as eldest Grandson Bart recalls, the barn and haymow don't seem nearly as large and looming now as they did when we were youngsters.

Farther to the east were the hog house, with one board missing over the door that I used for years as a basket for half-ears of corn in make-shift basketball; a tattered corn crib; and a squat, leaky granary. All had different shades of paints in years long since remote. The hog house feeding floor had a trough with one end missing; fortunately, the feeding floor was at an angle so the water collected in one end of the trough. In the middle of that feeding floor was a big hole broken in the concrete — and it's still there.

A grove thick enough that grass didn't grow in it back in the 1940s lay on the west and northwest sides of the yards. A tornado that tore through the yards in 1969 helped decimate much of the grove. Daddy said the water well was 220 feet deep, one of the three deepest in the neighborhood, and the water tasted wonderful. The yards were a mess.

Mother and Daddy went to work. Lynn Bauer wired the place for electricity — pretty ineptly. With Steve Burnett's help, Daddy built a chicken house across from the shop. Daddy was very fussy about always having his machinery and his car inside at night, so he built a machine shed next to the windmill with two big doors at each end. While in the service, Chuck paid $300 to have running water installed, and Daddy took down the windmill. He put new stanchions in the east side of the cow barn for the ill-fated new herd. He put up a silo with the help of Charley Lantz, an old friend; regrettably, he only filled it a few times. The shop, corn crib, and granary are gone now — I helped tear them down and I'm sorry about that. One slab of the corn crib floor is in my front yard and I never move it to mow my lawn without feeling a tug in my throat. What Daddy did not get done, however, was the painting of the buildings. So that became some of my summer projects. In 1949 I found in the shop a five-gallon tin of red paint, so old that it was like thick mud. I got linseed oil, mixed and mixed until it got thin enough to spread and started in on the buildings for their first coat in years and years. In 1953 Harold and I gave the buildings another coat; in 1966 we painted the buildings a very bright red. One time we got spray guns and did the entire set of buildings in a day. Although a recent trip home revealed that we never did get the north side of the barn done completely even once.

The house was a typical structure now about 100 years old. The house centered on the Dining Room looking out over the yard. The wall between two smaller rooms had been taken out to form a large living room which we called the Front Room. I loved that room, with its five wall lamps. Off the dining room to the north was a small kitchen, and a back porch in the L framed by the dining room and the kitchen. Off the Dining Room to the south was the Front Porch in the L formed by the Dining Room and the Front Room.

None of the floors was the same level. We had to walk up or down a small step when going from one room to the next until Daddy put in mini ramps in the doorways. At first there were pot-belly stoves in the Dining Room and Front Room, which Daddy would light, sometimes with the aid of a healthy dousing of gasoline on cobs, in the wintertime. Sometimes those fires burned so fast that the stove pipes extending up through the upstairs bedrooms were red hot, and I was afraid the house was going to burn down. Mother cooked with a wood-burning stove, heating water in the reservoir on the side, baking things with a fire that quickly flamed hot and cold, particularly if the fuel was cobs. One of our favorite dogs of all time, Nellie, a collie, would sleep behind the stove in the kitchen.

There were three bedrooms upstairs. In the master bedroom, overlooking the yard, were two double beds and two single beds, sleeping Mother and Daddy and Harriet and Harold. I cannot remember where I slept. In the South Room, overlooking the road and my favorite room in the house, Lois, Marie and later Harriet slept. In the tiny North Room, Chuck and Paul slept. And not a single closet in the whole house when Mother and Daddy moved in.

Paulette and Gary — and I, too — have wonderful memories of sleeping at the farm. "When I stay in a place that has heavy outside traffic," Paulette says, "I just think of the South Room. It faced Highway 18. When I remember its familiar surroundings, it's not as difficult to fall asleep." "I used to lie awake nights listening to the semis approach, roar past, and then purr into the distance," Gary recalls. "It was a strangely calming and peaceful experience, as if the world went on in its rhythms all night long so that I could sleep, resting up for my turn to contribute to the beat of the next day."

In 1940, a year after moving onto the place, the folks insulated the attic and put a gray but unattractive siding on the outside of the house. One of the first projects was to knock off the open front porch and add on a bedroom — which is still always called the Front Porch. Iver Berg, a brother-in-law of Grandma

Halsor and a carpenter, came out to install a new sink in the kitchen after the water system was installed. The Folks had wall-to-wall carpeting laid in the Front Room in February 1949. We thought it a big advance technologically that after we got running water, Daddy installed water pipes in the cook stove and heated water that way. Daddy built closets in the bedrooms. To save money, Mother painted and re-painted the linoleum in the kitchen and dining room and gave it a 'dappled' effect by rolling a crumpled rag with paint over it. During the early 1950s, nearly 15 years after moving in, the folks converted the North Room into a bath room. But the drain on the bathtub never did work satisfactorily, and to the end we had to keep it pried open with something.

While appraising for Cleminshaw, Daddy learned about gas wall furnaces, and he installed them. They rumbled and banged night and day. The grandchildren loved to play with the beaded chains that hung out the front and were used to regulate the air flow.

Some of the furniture I loved — the oak desk in the Dining Room and the oak library table with the iron-ring handles that I loved to flick. Mother had a buffet with a mirror in the Dining Room; in later years this gave way to a hutch. These now are in Harold's home.

A black walnut dresser and chiffonnier in the East Room, Mother and Daddy's bedroom, were the only things dating from the time they got married that were saved from the California fire.

Downstairs, the squeaky round dining table gave way in later years to a rectangular mahogany table with leaves that pulled out and five mahogany chairs for it. Mother and Daddy also got another buffet, of mahogany with a silverware drawer. All of these, along with a steamer trunk from Norway dated 1878, and two kitchen chairs and a dresser in the South Room of light wood, were refinished exquisitely by Dawn.

Grandpa and Grandma Pippert gave Mother and Daddy an upright piano that Dawn has dated to 1910 to 1920. We always considered it a high-quality instrument. Paul, Marie, Harriet, and Harold spent hours and hours at it. Mother always put greeting cards that she received on top of the piano. The sofa from the Front Room, on which I spent some of the most restful times in my life, was reupholstered by Marie. I took the main dresser from the South Room and refinished it. The drawers still pull out hard. Mother also had a four-wheel tea cart that somehow, she gave to Rev. Tieszen.

Mother had created a showcase by walling off the window between the Dining Room and the Front Porch. Here she kept her collection of cups. She must have had 50 or 60 cups and saucers. Children, grandchildren, friends and neighbors all contributed — and now share the collection. Roy, for instance, brought her one from every state he had been to — and thus there were cups marked Tennessee, Florida, Kentucky, Indiana.

Meanwhile, Mother was more than busy around the yards. She planted zinnias, sweet peas, cock's combs, iris, grape vines and all kinds of things around the house, and soon there was a back yard that I doubt was equaled anywhere in the county in terms of the flowers. Mother and Daddy put in apple trees, a grape arbor and a row of rhubarb behind the house, and between the house and the driveway, a mammoth garden with a huge strawberry bed and an even bigger patch of raspberries. What they couldn't raise, they bought and canned. Every July there were crates of peaches under the bed in the front porch. Before the end of the month, they'd be sealed up in Ball jars and neatly stored on shelves in the cellar, or she and Daddy might buy 'a lug' of bing cherries to can. In later years the canning was supplanted by a big freezer in the back porch. It was always chock full.

As for the fields, there were several, all fenced in with rusty, faulty fencing. Directly to the north of the buildings was the pasture, which Daddy soon broke. A lane led north from the west edge of the grove to the new pasture. A draw came down from Calvin's 80 and sliced the northwest corner of the farm; Daddy converted it to pasture to eliminate the erosion. Gradually, Daddy took out the fences to make bigger fields, requiring less turn-around time. Just east of the cornfield there was a big stone — about 3 feet in diameter — that would make Daddy's big 3-16 plow (three bottoms, 16-inch plow blades) almost jump out of the ground when we would hit it. Now that stone occupies a place of honor in my front yard.

I used to think that Daddy spanned a tremendous period in his life, from horse and buggy to car to jets and television. I now realize that the revolution has been greater in my lifetime — from the last team of horses to computers of unfathomed capability.

Daddy's last team of horses were named Dick and Pearl. One day Pearl died in the harness out in the field. Dick neighed mournfully all night. The next morning, Daddy took Dick out to the field and the horse sniffed his fallen mate. After that, he neighed no more. Later, with Dick and Pearl gone, down came the horse barn. I thought this was progress at the time, but now it just makes me nostalgic and a little sad to think about it. In the early 1940s, Daddy had two tractors — a 22-36 McCormick-Deering plow tractor, and an F12 Farm-All for cultivating. During the war he managed to get a new John Deere A.

The 22-36 was a mountain of a machine, with lug wheels. Mother was operating it to break up the old pasture north of the buildings in the early 1940s when she ran into barbed wire that tangled the plow. It was the nearest I saw her to being outright provoked. Both Paul and I broke our arms cranking the old McCormick-Deering, but Paul had the added thrill of rolling the new John Deere with his arm still in a cast.

When Daddy began appraising in Black Hawk County in 1949, he sold the A to a farmer near there, and later he got a smooth-sounding International M. Daddy also got an Allis Chalmers combine during the 1940s, and our threshing machine slowly rotted away in the grove. Daddy had a 10-foot power binder — the only one in the neighborhood that was not an 8-foot wheel-driven binder. Occasionally he would do 'custom work', cut the Grubens' oats or whatever. I would drive for him when he did this, proud of those sharp right-angle turns I executed. The binder always occupied a position of honor in the northeast corner of the machine shed.

Daddy always milked 12 or 15 cows, either milking by hand or with a DeLaval milking machine he bought. He strained the milk into 10-gallon cans and put it in the stock tank to cool. Every morning, Jack Williams would come by in his Ford V-8 slat box truck to pick up the two or three 10-gallon cans. And every two weeks, Daddy would get $40 or $50 in cash from Williams' Sweet Clover Dairy. He loved to skim off some of the thick cream in the 10-gallon cans and put on fresh strawberries or raspberries. He would farrow eight or ten sows, with maybe 50 or 60 pigs, feed them out over six or seven months, and sell them either direct to Jacob E. Decker & Sons packing plant in Mason City, or more likely, to Johnson hog buyers.

Mother, meanwhile, always had 300 chickens, generally raising them from baby chicks. She would sell eggs by the case to Sam Raizes Department store to be candled — that is, insert the eggs one by one into a hole in a brightly lit box in order to determine freshness — and she would 'dress' chickens to sell to the Soda Grill or other restaurants in Mason City. The eggs that Mother sold kept our family in groceries and clothes from Sam Raizes, but I still seem to remember that we generally had a $50 to $100 bill at Sam Raizes.

I remember being out in the yard near the grinder on Sunday, Dec. 7, 1941, when Mother and Lois came out to tell Daddy that the Japs had attacked

Pearl Harbor. He looked shocked. I thought, so what's the big deal about that? So many of the early years were war years: gasoline was rationed, down to one or two gallons a week (one had to mount an 'A', 'B', or 'C' in the car window to show how much gas you were entitled to); two pairs of shoes a year; a half-pound of sugar a week; and you needed coupon books to buy all kinds of things. Daddy came up with the intelligence that you could find syrup by checking under a certain shelving area at National Tea and A&P, the only two supermarkets in Mason City. With the war effort in mind, and Chuck in the service, Daddy did his part by putting in ten acres of hemp. The hemp was harvested and taken to a wartime hemp plant just west of Mason City to make rope. It probably was marijuana.

The winters were, in short, horrible. Those were before the days of parkas and we wore mackinaws that were little more than heavy cloth. Daddy picked corn by hand as a young man, and I can still remember his doing so a few times later. Then came the days of the tractor, the operator's seat totally exposed in the frigid winter winds, pulling a single- or double-row corn picker. How they ever kept from freezing to death is beyond me.

Our most memorable Christmas was that in 1946, the first Christmas Chuck was home from the war. The presents were piled half-way up the Christmas tree in the front room. Both Daddy and Chuck decided unawares to give each other the same thing — a toolbox. Chuck wrapped his; but Daddy, with his occasional burst of flare, simply wanted to hand Chuck his.

Beyond that Daddy was a good neighbor. Our favorite neighbors were Hugh and Jesse Hughes, who moved into the first place west when the Hartmans moved off and closed their dairy. Jesse was a Krause, whom Mother had taught, and Hugh was the only farmer in the neighborhood with a degree from Iowa State. They had three children, Frank, who became a veterinarian, Helen, a dietician, and Joan, a nurse. Helen had diabetes and she died at 25, and I was one of her pallbearers. We really liked the Hughes.

As I write this, I see now how hard the folks worked. We all know Mother worked hard; Daddy didn't talk about it as much, but he obviously was working hard, too. Superimposed on all this, of course, were the activities at the Alliance Gospel Tabernacle and in the Portland community. It made for a full life.

We never worked on Sunday, and, in fact, one test of whether a neighbor was a Christian was whether he worked in the fields on Sunday. Maybe one in three did. Mother rarely if ever shopped; Daddy never went in the fields. The habit stuck. I went all through Iowa, Wheaton, and Harvard and never studied on Sunday — not once. Paul, of course, put his own twist on it. "I don't work on Sunday either," he used to say. "It's not that I think it's wrong; I just don't want to work." Paul, the least lazy of men.

Aside from Sunday night church (if Frank Emmert was visiting, he and the Folks would talk about the imminence of the Second Coming), radio station KGLO provided our evening entertainment, or CBS ("This is CBS, the Columbia Broadcasting System"). One problem, however, was our radio, a Philco, I believe. The tuning knob didn't work so we had to reach into it from behind and turn the tuning wheel with our fingers, generally burning our hand on the hot tubes in the process.

Daddy's favorite program was 'The Aldrich Family', whose son Henry got into one pickle after another, and 'Blondie'. Daddy always laughed uproariously when Blondie would hold open the door for Dagwood and he would "WHOOOOOSH" out and the door would slam shut. Now and then we would catch the hour-long 'Lux Radio Theatre' or 'Inner Sanctum' on Monday night, or the 'Hit Parade' on Saturday night. I listened to the equivalent of kid 'soaps'. One of them was 'Wilderness Lane', which came on the air on CBS at 4:45 p.m. I was listening to it when John Daly broke in on April 12, 1945, to announce that Franklin D. Roosevelt was dead. I was 10 but I knew the implications of that, and I went out in the yard to tell Mother.

But how we children played! We played hide-and-seek in the grove, and I imagined how fun it would be to play it as an adult. From the time country school let out in May until it resumed in September we went barefoot, barely tiptoeing across Daddy's cinder driveway at first and then sprinting across by the end of the summer. Occasionally one of us would step on a nail; Mother would put on a poultice of a strip of bacon.

The long summer nights seemed to last an eternity. They were quiet, except for the crickets and the occasional haunting hoot of an owl. We children played until past dark and then we would go in the house. It is a nostalgia so precious that it is now almost painful to recall.

The decades moved along. Lois was away at St. Paul Bible Institute and actually lived on the farm a short time only; she graduated in City High School 1943. Chuck and Paul graduated from Mason in 1942; Chuck joined the Navy that October, but the folks got Paul farm deferments and he put off his military service until 1946. Marie graduated from country school in 1943, and rode the bus to Nora Springs High School, graduating in 1947, then going on to SPBI a year later. I graduated from country school in 1947 and Mason City High School in 1951. And then off to the University of Iowa at 17. So, actually, my year-round experience on the Old J.H. Pippert farm was only 12 years in length.

The last remaining three, 10 November 2019. Marie, Harold, and I met at the Mason City Hy-Vee after Aunt Wava's funeral. Later this evening, Marie would have a heart attack. She died four months later.

I seemed to have a psychic need to spend more time there and I spent college summers and for several years my four- and five-week annual UPI vacations at home, loving it.

Even as we began to scatter, we children kept coming home often. The entry for Sunday, December 3, 1950, says: "Dad, I went to church. Paul & Wava came later. Marie, Roy, Paul, Wava were here for dinner. Chuck & Billie came over in the evening. I went to the Messiah. Roy, Marie & Lois to the Choral Club in Osage. Paul left for Shenandoah." There were lots of entries like that.

Mother, the city girl, stayed alone on the farm for three years after Daddy died. When Harold finally got an apartment for her in the Manor, the old Hotel Hanford, he phoned Marie where Mother was at the time. When she heard the word, she cried for it meant she was leaving for good what was really her home, the farm. The weekend she moved in, her only surviving family member, her brother Al, died. It was too bad because they would only have lived a few blocks apart.

Now, in the front yard rests a big stone with a bronze marker put there by Roy:

> Harry and Magda Pippert
> moved onto this farm on March 1, 1939.
> They tilled the soil and raised their children
> and grandchildren with a firm belief in God.
> This is dedicated in their memory. March, 1984.

Appendix

CHRONOLOGY

1895 Mother is born.

1897 Daddy is born.

1914 Mother graduates from Mason City High School. About this time, Grandpa and Grandma Pippert moved off the Old J.H. Pippert farm, later our home place, to the Old Krause farm, where Bob Krause now lives.

1914-1921 Mother teaches at Portland 2, 1914-1915; Portland 3, 1915-16; Portland 6, 1916-1919; Hanlontown, 199-1920; Burchinal, 1920.

1919 Daddy helps harvest in Canada near Winnipeg.

1920 Mother and Daddy are married.

1921 Lois is born in a stone house on the Pike, near what became Taylor Bridge and US 18. About this time, Grandpa and Grandma Pippert move to the Selle farm, which later became the site of MacNiders' mansion.

1922-1927 Folks live in California.

1924 Chuck is born.

1925 Paul is born in Talbot, Calif.

1927 Folks return from California and move to Gage place along the Winnebago River. They move in the next few years to the Krieger or Felt Place and south of Emory. Grandpa Pippert sells the Selle place to the MacNiders and they built the Indianhead mansion there.

1930 Marie is born on a farm south of Emory.

1931 Folks move onto Ladwig place.

1934 Wesley is born.

1937 Harriet is born. Grandpa and Grandma Pippert retire and move from the Old Ladwig place, where the Bartletts later lived, to the Millington acreage near Mason city.

1938 Daddy buys the home place.

1939 Mother and Daddy move from the Ladwig place to the home place. Harold is born. Cousin Ernestine and Junior marry.

1940 The folks insulate the house.

1942 Chuck and Paul graduate from Mason City High School, and Chuck joins the U.S. Navy. Grandpa Charles Pippert dies at 76.

1943   Lois graduates from St. Paul Bible Institute and marries James Comstock. Lowell Young comes to Mason city as pastor.

1944   Lois' first child, Barry, is born in Mason City.

1945   Paul starts his career in radio at KWAT, Watertown, S.D.

1946   Paul enters the army. Chuck is discharged from the navy and returns home to start farming. Mother suffers her first heart attack. Lois' No. 2, Jay, is born. Great-uncle Lou Pelzer dies at 67.

1947   Jim and Lois go to Colombia as missionaries. Their No. 3, Laurence, is born. Marie graduates from Nora Springs High School and Wesley from Portland No. 2.

1948   Daddy appraises in Cerro Gordo County. Chuck and Billy get married. KSMN goes on the air with Paul a member of its maiden staff.

1949   Mother takes Harold and Harriet with her to visit Grandpa Halsor in California. Daddy appraises in Black Hawk (Waterloo) County. Lois' No. 4, Dale, and Chuck's No. 1, Richard, are born. Wesley paints the buildings. Folks carpet the Front Room. We get a black chow puppy. Next-door neighbor Pete Steil dies at 86.

1950   Roy and Marie get married. The family takes a rare overnight trip, staying at Violet's in Minburn, Iowa, en route to visit Paul in Shenandoah. Julene Adelsman, Mervyl Williams, Harriett Hert, Marcheta Rodberg, Beverly Carr all graduate from Mason City High School in a mammoth Alliance class. C.D. Tieszen replaces Lowell Young as Alliance pastor. Paul Behm succeeds Carleton Stewart as high school band director.

1951   Paul and Wava get married. Wesley graduates from Mason City High School. Chuck's No. 2, Gregory, and Paul's daughter Paulette, are born. Death: churchwoman Anna Douglas, 78.

1952   Marie's eldest, Gordon, is born on Harriet's 15th birthday, the same day Grandma Halsor is buried. Cousin Jovetta dies at 26: second cousin Amanda, daughter of Aunt Bertha Halsor Larson: Billy's father, William Poppen, 67; Gladys Elfstrand, 45: Aunt Phyllis' brother Francis Letts, 50. Churchman-neighbor Carl Claus is killed in action in Korea. Paul, Marie, and Harold vacation in the Black Hills. Tatum's Hardware of Nora Springs installs new sink in the kitchen.

1953   Daddy appraises in Nebraska City. Mother is president of the Ladies Mission Band at the Alliance church. Harriet spends time in the hospital. At Auntie Esther's suggestion, Billy arranges for us children to buy Mother a Lazy Susan for her birthday. Lois' first daughter, Brooke, is born. Paul and Wava vacation in the Wyoming Big Horn Mountains. Wesley and Harold paint the buildings, complete with trim. Harriet spends a lengthy time in the hospital. The Alliance church moves out of the 'tabernacle' at 616 N Delaware. Mason City's centennial. Deaths: Next-door neighbor Helen Hughes, 25; silo-salesman Charles Lantz, 65.

1954   This is a difficult year at home. Mother has surgery and recuperates at Auntie Esther's; Harriet has a two-month buildup to prepare her for surgery that removes an internal goiter. Mother and Harriet visit Lois and Jim in Kansas City. Paul joins KCMO in Kansas City. Marie's No. 2 son, Gary, is born. Great-uncle Will Freese, 82, dies. Portland 2 school closes for good. The paving of new US 18 past the farm begins. Uncle Les buys the '110' acre place on old US 18 for $26,000, with $2,600 down and $1,000 a year. He also breaks ground for a new Alliance church in Mason city. Churchman John Glandon dies at 79; neighbor Carrie Felt, 89.

1955   Another difficult year at home: Grandpa becomes seriously ill in California in June, Mother goes out, and he moves back to Iowa, only to return to California in October. Lois' youngest, Paige, is born. Chuck buys a farm near Stewartville, Minn. Wesley graduates from University of Iowa. Neighbor Frank Krause dies at 92. New US 18 past the farm opens. New Calvary Alliance Church is dedicated.

1955-1959   Lois and Jim are in Brazil with the oriental Missionary society.

1956   Mother and Daddy went on perhaps their first vacation in many years — for three days. Harriet graduates from Nora Springs High School. Marie's only daughter, Dawn Marie, is born. Deaths: Hanford pastor Gordon Loucks, 48.

1957   Mother, Daddy, and Wesley visit Lois and Jim in Indiana. Wesley becomes lay pastor of the Methodist churches in Blunt-Harrold, South Daktoa, while on assignment with UPI in Pierre. Harriet attends St. Paul Bible Institute. Harold graduates from Mason City High School. Tornado rips some Kansas City suburbs.

1958-1960   Mother is president of the Alliance Missionary Prayer Band.

1958   Mother visits Grandpa Halsor in California. Harriet undergoes examination at University Hospitals in Iowa City and is sent to the Independence State Hospital. Chuck's youngest, Janet Sue, and Marie's youngest, Douglas, are born. Paul joins the farm-market staff at KCMO, Kansas City. Daddy takes down the old corn crib. Harold works on the gang rerouting and paving US 18 past our farm. Deaths: Second cousin Audrey Freese, 48, in a car accident at Taylor Bridge, and our teacher Norleda Sandy, 49, and neighbor Elmer Krause, 65.

1959   Mother and Daddy and Uncle Calvin and Aunt Mabel take a trip to the Ozarks by way of Paul and Wava in Kansas City. Mother is president of the Ladies Missionary band. Lois and Jim and family arrive home from South America. Daddy and Wesley ride in a chartered plane hours before the same pilot crashes with it, killing Buddy Holly, Richie Valens and the Big Bopper, J.P.Richardson. Other deaths: Churchwomen Shirley Glandon, 80, and Ellen Kinsel, 58.

1960   Mother and Daddy have a 40th anniversary celebration, the last time the nine of us were together. Daddy appraised in the Dubuque area. Paul has back surgery. Roy and Marie leave Oconomowoc, Wisconsin, pastorate for Wheaton. Deaths: Neighbor Billy Krause, 31; former pastor L.A. Perkins, 66; churchmen Sidney Snell, 53, and Otto Dahl, 77.

1961   Chuck dies at 36; Grandma Pippert, 87, and Cousin Marilyn, 23, also pass away. Daddy appraises near Dubuque and Benton Harbor, Michigan. Wesley is transferred from Pierre to Chicago and moves in with Marie and Roy. Harold tears down the granary and he and Wesley paint the buildings. Deaths: Churchwoman Ida Hert, 62.

1962   Daddy appraises in Michigan and Johnson County, Iowa. Mother has back surgery. Paul is president of the Kansas City Livestock Market Boosters Club. Harold serves in the U.S. Army. Paul and Wesley negotiate a deal with Cerro Gordo county for Harriet's care.

1963   Daddy appraises in Cerro Gordo and Worth counties and assesses in Falls Township. Paul edits *Chats*, the publication of the National Association of Farm Broadcasters and takes part in a C.S. Lewis drama at his church in Prairie Village. A good crop year. Uncle Al retires after 46 years with First National Bank.

1964   Daddy appraises in Cerro Gordo and Hancock counties, and Keokuk. Marie starts work at Wheaton's Conservatory of Music, and she and Roy buy their house in Wheaton at 714 E Illinois. Paul takes 6,500-mile trip west. Wesley makes his first trip abroad, including an archaeological dig on the west bank of the Jordan River. Harold's eldest Todd is born.

1965   Grandpa Halsor dies and is buried on his 96th birthday. Daddy appraised in Sioux, Clinton, and Franklin counties. Lois graduated from Friends University, and she and Jim go to the Orient for three months. Harold works at Waverly as an Armour hog buyer. Deaths: Mrs. Comstock, Jim and Roy's mother, in a car accident at 76; Great-aunt Ella Pippert Freese at 87; and neighbors Emmert brothers Frank, 76, and Ben, 78, and Lynn Bauer, 60.

1966   Mother is president of the County WCTU. Daddy appraised in Humboldt and Webster counties. Wesley and Roy get their master's degrees from Wheaton, and Wesley gets a Congressional Fellowship in Washington. Harold and Sandy marry. Bart graduates from Taylor. Harold and Wesley paint the buildings, including the barn a bright red. Deaths: Neighbors Esther Tevis, 73, and Hank Gruben, 60.

1967   Daddy has cardiac arrest at Methodist Hospital while at Mayo Clinic for cancer on his voice box. He recovers completely from both. Paul wins National Future Farmers' Distinguished Service Award and graduates from Reisch School of Auctioneering. Harold and Roy tear down the shop-cob shed. Bella and Shirley celebrate their 50th anniversary. Bart and Marilyn marry. Harold's Annette is born. C.D. Tieszen leaves Mason City as pastor. Chancellor V. Raymond Edman dies during chapel talk at Wheaton.

1968   Wesley serves as Sen. Charles H. Percy's press aide, and after the Republican National Convention in Miami Beach, he and Paul vacation on Key West. Second-cousin Marcia Methus marries Bill Young.

1969   Daddy appraises in Wright, Iowa (Marengo) and Clinton counties. A tornado destroys much of the grove. Harold buys old Files place south of Portland. Monique Janee is born to nephew Bart and Marilyn. Aunt Bella dies at 73 and Uncle Carl's brother Bob Haase, 53. North Iowa Area Community College moves to new campus on Uncle Calvin's old farm.

1970   Mother and Daddy celebrate their 50th anniversary, as do neighbors Herman and Helen Diercks, Harry and Stella Bisgrove, Fred and Dorothy Mallo, and mailman Milt and Ione Lewis. Paul is elected regional vice president of the National Association of Farm Broadcasters. Bart gets his M.D. from Kansas University. Jay and Shirley marry. Paulette is honored queen of the Job's Daughters. Deaths: Daddy's teachers Gertrude Macleod Bauer, 91, and Maude currier Emmert, 81; Mother's friend Ella Essex, 82; churchman Jeff Billick at 82; neighbor Susie Billings at 66, seedman William Sinnard at 93.

1971   Harold goes to Colombia on short-term mission project. Kimberly Faye is born to nephew Jay and Shirley. Deaths: Aunt Ruth, 62, churchman Jeff Billick, 82.

1972 Wava's mother dies at 69. Harold's son Jason is born. Paul goes to Munich Olympics. Wesley covers the first of three presidential campaigns. Neighbor Rosetta Dunlap dies. Mother is hit by a tailgater as she slows to turn into the farm's driveway at 77, the end of her driving.

1973 Paul becomes KCMO farm director. Nephew Larry and Faye get married. Nephew Jay graduates from Asbury Seminary. Uncle Les dies at 59. Cerro Gordo County Supervisor J.C. Dickinson dies at 77.

1974 Angela Denise is born to nephew Jay and Shirley. Nephew Gordon graduates from Wheaton. Doc Bascom leaves Nora Springs.

1974-1975 Aunt Esther, 72, Aunt Phyllis and Uncle Shirley, 79, die within a 13-month period, and neighbors Price Tevis, 83, Hugh Hughes, 77, Clarence Steil, 79, and his sister Alma Thogerson, 81, and neighbor (and Lois' teacher?) Hilda McEachran, 82; Mason City contractor Carl Henkel, 79; and churchmen Ivan Wendt, 76, and a day apart, Harvey Green, 90, and Thelma Dahl Pietersen, 63.

1975 Roy and Marie celebrate their silver anniversary with their children at Deer Valley Ranch, Colorado. Wesley goes to the University of Michigan on a National Endowment for the Humanities Fellowship. Niece Brooke and Ed Bruner and Nephew Greg and Linda Pippert marry. Harold's Jennifer is born. Sandy's niece Brenda Cordle dies at 13. Jacob E. Decker & Sons packing plant closes down.

1976 Daddy dies, and within a few weeks former pastor Paul Freligh, fellow churchman Joe Adelsman, and former neighbor Wilbur Kellogg also pass away. Paul goes to Eastern Europe. Wesley covers Carter campaign for UPI and then is assigned to the White House. Nephew Gary Comstock and Karen Werner, and niece Paulette and Greg Cott marry.

1977 P.C. Hamilton dies and Wesley gives the eulogy. Flood strikes Kansas City. Daddy's eye doctor C.C. Chenoweth dies at 86.

1978 Wesley and Becky marry. Nephew Richard gets his master's degree from Scarritt.

1979 Mother leaves the farm to live at the Manor in the old Hanford Hotel in Mason City, and Uncle Alfred dies the same weekend. Paul visits China. Cousin Louise dies at 36.

1980 Paul has back surgery. Sandy's parents, the Ballhagens, celebrate their 50th wedding anniversary.

1983 Mother dies. Several of us buy the "80" that Uncle Calvin farmed north of our farm for so long. Paul visits Scandinavia and Hungary. Wesley

	is transferred by UPI to Israel. Harold is elected to board of Portland elevator.
1984	Paul visits Israel.
1985	Daughter Elizabeth Marie is born in Jerusalem.
1986	Lois passes away at 64. Paul visits Israel. Wesley and Becky return from Israel; son David is born in Boston. 1987 Paul wins Ciba-Geigy Chemicals trip to Switzerland as the "outstanding farm broadcaster of the year." Wesley spends year as Fellow at Harvard. Sandy gets degree in special education from Buena Vista. Neighbor Glen McEachran dies, 94.
1988	Niece Heather is Miss Nora Springs in the North Iowa Band Festival. Uncle Earl, 86, and churchman Vernon Dahl die on the same weekend.
1989	Wava becomes first woman to win the National Association of Farm Broadcasters' Meritorious Service Award. Wesley becomes director of the University of Missouri's Washington Reporting Program. Nephew Larry graduates from North Texas State.
1990	Churchman Virgil Carr and Margery Hert die.

Daddy's Letter to His Family

St. Joseph, Michigan December 18, 1961

To my sister and Brothers,

    To all of us sooner or later there comes a time of separating, the parting of loved ones. So it has come to us. We children have now laid to rest our Father and Mother. Our time of separation has come. How soon it will be for one of us is not for us to say, but it may be sooner than we think. So as the time has come, what was our home until just a short time ago is now broken and we don't have that home anymore. It was our Mother's desire the division of her things should be done very peaceably, and I think that was the wish of us children.

    I'm sure these parents of ours did what they thought best. They were common people who tried to teach us right from wrong, to be honest peaceable children. We were all taken to church and Sunday School without fail, to respect the rights of others, and, as Mother wished, that we should be an unbroken circle on the other side.

    Now a little look in our father's business dealings since about 1919. That year he sold the old Krause farm, 145 acres. For $33,000 (perhaps some of these dates and figures could be a little wrong but I will try and be somewhere near the line). Then he rented the old Selle farm. About December he decided to buy the farm instead of renting, some over $55,000. He only had the farm about a week and a businessman in Mason City offered him $1,500 profit and the crop of 1921. But Dad turned it down. He only paid down $15000, so he was paying interest on the balance of the mortgage. But Dad loaned his money out at eight per cent.

    Father carried on for some years, until 1927, when he got to the place, at least he thought so, where he was going to lose the farm! (I might add right here that our Father and Mother had inherited between $18,000 and $20,000 — give or take a little, one way or the other.) MacNider rented the farm, and he had our Dad rather spellbound. Well, in July 1927, he came to me and said, "I'm going to sell the farm as I will lose it." (Sometime before that he had told me that if Mother and I would put our money in the farm we could reduce the mortgage to $4,500 or $5,000, give or take.) I asked him to reconsider the deal, but as I found out later, it was already sold.

Well, March 1st, 1928, came. Dad went up to get his $15,000 that he had paid in 1920. But when MacNider got through that day, we only went home with $7,000 — MacNider made him take off $8,000. Likewise Mr. Selle on his mortgage. He had to cut off $10,000. $18,000 on one farm in one day — pretty good day's wages. That was the year that they moved the buildings down the road. Again, he really clipped poor old Dad, but Dad wouldn't take any of us along, so he took it!

Now, back to March 1st. He took his money and let Beck have some. Several of the businessmen of Mason City signed the papers. (How much money at that year I don't know.) This money was shifted from one mortgage to another, Dad was very slack and the first thing, his papers were outlawed. Up to this time Mr. Beck had paid Dad 123 percent on the loan. Something was wrong and why those at home didn't catch it, we don't know. I talked with Calvin one day about it, so after several talks, he admitted the mortgage papers and notes had gotten to the place where they were outlawed.

So I went to Mr. Beck with the matter and the first thing he told me was, "Harry, the papers are outlawed and you don't have a leg to stand on." I admitted it. But I said, "Father and Mother's life savings are all wrapped up here," and I said, "Do you think this is just right?" Then he said, "If it weren't for you and Magda, I wouldn't waste my time. *But*, if you and I can work this out I'll do something."

After a lot of lost time: from the farm and my work we inherited the properties you all remember.

Not long after this Father passed away; one hot July day in 1942. Father had made out a will. Mother had life estate on all the properties, bond, etc. But she at once broke the will (here I will add that Calvin was put in as administrator of father's estate without pay, and had to pay his own bond. I still think he should be paid).

And Mother at once started to sell the different properties, which, according to the will, belonged to us children. She also sold her country home at a very low price. In the meantime, Mr. Beck told me not to be in a hurry to sell the three tracts. But we couldn't convince Mother, so she sold. Two years later we could have doubled our money.

She then bought the house on 111 7th for a given amount. The day she bought she borrowed $500 from Calvin for down payment. I saw the check written and I also saw where she gave him back the $500 within a period of 20 days. The country home had been sold but was in process at that time.

No mortgage or anything, just a loan. This was about two years after Dad passed away.

Now my own affairs with Dad. When I bought the farm, he wondered if he could leave his share in the farm, thereby get a little more interest. It was agreed. I kept my interest paid. When Mother started dividing money, she only gave me credit on my account. We'll say here after I got all those properties in Dad's name from Mr. Beck: our old Dad gave me $5…

Now a few words about Mother. It was hard for her to handle money, and with all she had through the years, she did a lot of talking of no money. We have all paid, some more than others. At the time we put the siding on the house, we had gotten a $125 check from Mrs. Hettler(?) which was used to help put on the siding. It was to be all donated labor. Earl brought his two carpenters, so that we could get it on.

Leslie helped paint, while we three older ones helped outside. Now back in 1961. We received another check of $200 which was put to her account, part of it went to pay her plane trip to Dayton.

Personally, I have no ill feeling to my sister and her husband, or any of my brothers or their wives, but have thought many times if we only could all join together instead of the way things are.

I've not gone too much into detail but thought some of these things should be brought out, so all know about some of the dealings that were made. A lot of them haven't been mentioned at all. If anyone has any questions on this little paper that I'm passing on, I will be glad to answer if possible.

Now this being December month, I want to wish my Sister, Brother-in-law, Brothers and Sisters-in-law a very Merry Christmas and Happy New Year. I hope no sorrow this next year.

Love to each one of you,
/s/ Harry

www.ingramcontent.com/pod-product-compliance
Lightning Source LLC
Chambersburg PA
CBHW081429070526
44586CB00020B/2529